CULTURE SHOCK!

A Student's Guide

GUEK-CHENG PANG
ROBERT BARLAS

Graphic Arts Center Publishing Company
Portland, Oregon

In the same series

Australia	*Ireland*	*Spain*	*A Globe-Trotter's Guide*
Bolivia	*Israel*	*Sri Lanka*	*A Traveller's Medical Guide*
Borneo	*Italy*	*Sweden*	*A Wife's Guide*
Britain	*Japan*	*Switzerland*	*Working Holidays Abroad*
Burma	*Korea*	*Syria*	
Canada	*Malaysia*	*Taiwan*	
China	*Morocco*	*Thailand*	
Denmark	*Nepal*	*Turkey*	
France	*Norway*	*United Arab Emirates*	
Germany	*Pakistan*	*USA*	
Hong Kong	*Philippines*	*USA—The South*	
India	*Singapore*	*Vietnam*	
Indonesia	*South Africa*		

Illustrations by TRIGG

This book is published by special
arrangement with Times Editions Pte Ltd
Times Centre, 1 New Industrial Road, Singapore 536196
International Standard Book Number 1-55868-244-9
Library of Congress Catalog Number 95-79459
Graphic Arts Center Publishing Company
P.O. Box 10306 • Portland, Oregon 97210 • (503) 226-2402

Printed in Singapore

To my son, Richard, whose time at McGill has proven to be both productive and useful in more ways than one!
—Robert Barlas

To Xavier and the future.
—Guek-Cheng Pang

CONTENTS

INTRODUCTION

One hot August day in Singapore, the two authors of this book sat down with their editor and tried to decide what should go between its covers. It soon became obvious that talking about studying overseas is a bit like talking about making love—most people have thought about doing it at some time in their lives, but the combination of circumstances has to be just right for each individual to get the maximum satisfaction out of doing it.

Physical surroundings, nationality, gender, opportunity, money, qualifications and just plain luck all play a part in any successful experience and the exact combination of all these can be as variable as the individuals themselves. As a result, when trying to discuss studying overseas, it is almost impossible to provide the specific information which each potential student from every country might need when considering studying in another one.

In putting together the book, we have sought the opinion of counsellors, foreign students past and present and those who have been intimately involved in international education. In all ways, we have tried to be as generic as possible in the information we provide: to look at the experience of studying overseas from the viewpoint of getting there, living there and, hopefully, graduating there. The information that we share with you, the examples we use to illustrate its various aspects and the experiences of past and present students that we have drawn upon will be relevant to you, no matter where you are going.

Robert Barkas & Guek-Cheng Pang

Chapter One

STUDYING OVERSEAS— IS IT FOR ME?

When you go overseas to study, you are joining the ranks of over a million foreign students in the world, according to figures given by UNESCO (the United Nations Educational, Scientific and Cultural Organisation).

You have behind you a long history that dates back to as early as the Middle Ages. Even then, there were already many foreign students at the Universities of Bologna and Paris such that these universities were known as *studia generalia*, meaning "places resorted to by scholars from all parts".

You may ask why there was ever a need for people to travel beyond the borders of their countries to get a good education. Well, with countries always at different stages of economic and cultural development, some having universities and others not, students travelled to get an education or to study at more famous schools than were available at home.

In the 19th century, German and French universities attracted many foreign students because of their reputation for scientific research. After the Second World War, there was a flow of postgraduate students to the United States because it excelled in the fields of science and technology.

With reconstruction taking place after the war, the richer countries agreed to help the poorer countries improve their educational standards as part of the fight against poverty and disease. The political security of the younger, newly independent countries was also vital for the survival of the western nations. There was an overall growth in higher education that coincided with the postwar increase in worldwide mobility. The developed countries sponsored overseas students and trained them so they could return home and contribute to their country's social and economic development. In addition, education and scholarship opportunities in developed countries were made available to unsponsored, private students.

The trend these days is for the majority of foreign students in higher education to study in the United States, France, Germany, the United Kingdom, Canada and what was formerly the USSR. In contrast, students from these six countries make up less than 10% of the total foreign student population worldwide, and they are enrolled mostly in universities in North America and Europe.

Most of today's foreign students are from Asia and Africa. Foreign students from Asia tend to choose to study in the United States and Canada, with a small percentage going to Europe. Many African students, on the other hand, go to France and the United States. Australia and New Zealand's percentage of the world's foreign student population is small, standing at less than 10%. Most of the students who choose to go to these two countries are from Asia.

Previously, the more developed European countries, North America, Australia and New Zealand provided education to overseas students at highly subsidised rates. In more recent years, the reduction in national income growth rates in these countries has resulted in a reappraisal of this policy. Unfortunately for many foreign students today, this means they often have to pay full fees. However, if the financial resources are available, this is not a deterrent as the numbers of foreign students are constantly growing for various reasons detailed in the next section. Indeed, there are signs that there will be further growth in the number of students enrolled in courses of higher education in foreign countries as universities and colleges, often cash-strapped and in search of new areas of funding, view foreign students as an important source of revenue and now actively market their courses abroad.

Canadian colleges and universities had a combined total of about 87,000 foreign students in 1990. Most of them were from Asia (56%), with students from other parts of North America making up 15%.

It has been projected that by the turn of the century, there may be more than one million foreign students in the United States.

THE REASONS

The most obvious reason for a student to go overseas to study is to get an education or training that is not available at home, or to obtain a diploma or degree from that particular country. Often, this is made necessary because there is stiff competition for places in their home universities. Some countries, for example, have only one or two universities to cater to a fairly large student population. For some other students, it is also the belief that a degree or diploma from a foreign university will further their career and give them added prestige.

It may also be that a particular university is well-known for a specific field of study, so that furthering one's knowledge in that field necessitates going there to get the best education possible. In some areas such as art history and architecture, there are special benefits in studying abroad as there is no substitute for learning from the real world instead of just gathering the information from books.

In western culture, it is a tradition for children of privileged families to go abroad to become acquainted with a broad range of cultural experiences and develop a wide understanding of the arts so as to become "cultured" citizens.

Many students who are part of an immigrant society may want to go overseas to study and, at the same time, find their roots, family and cultural heritage.

> *"One reason I went to the UK to study was that my family originated there and some of my relatives still live there. In going to the UK, I beat the travel bug students at university tend to get, but I still look forward to going somewhere else in the future."*
> —*ZQ, a Canadian*

Another reason is to study a language abroad, and to reach a better cultural understanding of the people whose language you are learning to speak. No matter how many hours of classroom study you have had in a language, there is no substitute for being immersed in the society of the people who speak the language. However, this can sometimes lead to embarrassing situations, as when a foreign student who looks similar to the natives of the country he or she is studying in is unable to speak the language fluently.

The plus point is that immersion in a new culture—and often a new language—widens the scope that studying offers, perhaps giving the individual student a long-awaited chance to experiment with a new perspective, or to refine and hone skills and ideas that may have been suppressed or stifled in surroundings that offer little by way of intellectual stimulation.

Sometimes, however, it is simply a case of wanting to live away from home, gain independence from the family or fulfil a desire for travel and new experiences. Everyone welcomes a change now and then, and students are no exception. How many people, gazing out of their bedroom windows on a bleak Monday morning, have wished themselves anywhere other than where they were at that moment—and it is at times like these when studying in another country seems to offer the opportunity for both escape and rejuvenation.

Studying in a new and different environment also offers the chance to try out new subjects and ideas and revitalise old ways of thinking. If a new educational challenge is the aim, changing one's personal and professional environment is certainly one way to go about it.

In addition to the personal and intellectual stimulation that studying abroad can bring in its wake, there are also many other reasons that have led students to choose to spend some time away from home. The opportunity for new friendships, new cultural experiences and new places to explore rank high among these, and all of them are available to the student who is willing to take the plunge. How valid these reasons are—and how far the hopes that they represent are fulfilled—is dependent on the individual and his true motivation for wanting to study overseas.

Any new experience is bound to bring about some degree of change in the people concerned and studying abroad is no exception. At the very least, there is a broadening in the way that a student looks at his area of study and its possibilities, and this can lead in turn to the recognition of new strengths and avenues for exploration.

Of the students who have attended overseas post-secondary institutions, most—if not all—found that their motivation to go did lead to an experience that enriched, stimulated and rejuvenated but, at the same time, also had the potential to frustrate and infuriate. Why you should study overseas is not a question which should be asked—or answered—lightly, but it is one that many students in the past have been forced to answer, and those who have come to a positive realisation of their personal motivation for going overseas have nearly always enjoyed the challenge that doing so posed, and the benefits that it offered.

THE SECRETS OF SUCCESS

Studying overseas is obviously a two-edged sword—it delights and frustrates, gives and takes away, rewards and punishes. In Robert Kohls' book, *Survival Kit for Overseas Living* (a useful guide for any student considering studying abroad), he lists the following skills which those who have lived overseas in a different country and culture seem to possess:

1. Tolerance for ambiguity
2. Low goal/task orientation
3. Open-mindedness
4. A non-judgmental attitude
5. Empathy
6. Communicativeness
7. Flexibility/adaptability
8. Curiosity
9. Sense of humour
10. Warmth in human relationships
11. Motivation
12. Self-reliance
13. Strong sense of self
14. Tolerance for differences
15. Perceptiveness
16. Ability to fail

Of these 16 traits, Dr. Kohls mentions having a sense of humour, a low goal/task orientation and the ability to fail as the three most important because they provide a built-in protection against failure in an overseas situation. They allow the individual to remain relaxed and ride with the unexpected things that may happen, keeping these in perspective instead of allowing them to ruin the whole experience.

THE BENEFITS

Many students who have studied overseas report that the experience acquired in a foreign country is the most important social and cultural reason for going to a foreign university. Likewise, you can expect a rewarding experience. After a period abroad, you will return home more mature, and culturally aware and sensitive. The experience will teach you to question your own prejudices and national stereotypes. It is good to observe, first-hand, how people in other cultures think differently and express their thoughts in ways that are different from yours. This is the broadening aspect of studying overseas.

As a foreign student, you will learn very quickly how to be independent because there are no family and friends upon whom to depend. You will have to make your own financial decisions regarding budgeting and living expenses, coping with your studies while cooking, cleaning and shopping at the same time. When you return home, you cannot but be more poised and self-possessed, ready to enter the next phase of your life.

Foreign students are an asset both at home and abroad. They are an important group of people in the country they go to. By interacting with other students, and with university staff and the society at large, they contribute to the knowledge of the host community. When they return home, they serve as a bridge between their home country and their host country. In many instances, these students return home to occupy important positions in government and business circles. The links they have formed will prove to be important later when building business contacts. Their experience will also be useful when drawing up or reviewing high-level corporate policies.

THE PITFALLS

Although the decision to study overseas has some glamorous—and practical—advantages, there are also disadvantages to be considered, and even some snares for the unwary and ill-prepared.

One thing studying overseas is never going to do is to help you solve problems. Going overseas to study is no solution for problems that already exist in the personal environment at home—support systems disappear, the new environment increases physical stresses (at least at first) and subtle challenges arise like vapours to test the strongest of personal identities. Before you decide to go and study overseas, make sure that those who will be going with you—or your loved ones who will be staying behind—are totally supportive of your move.

Without first resolving personal problems at home, the chances of studying overseas successfully are definitely diminished. The new environment has its own ways of testing newcomers. The biggest and most omnipresent of these is *unpredictability*. Most of us are creatures of habit and have ways of regulating our lives that make us feel comfortable and content. How will we react when these are taken from us, and we are not sure what to put in their place?

Being flexible and able to deal with crises as they occur—and they will—is a big part of being a successful student overseas, and those who find these things difficult to handle had better think carefully. Living and working in a new culture is, by its very nature, an unpredictable experience—it would be unwise, no matter how carefully you prepare before you leave, to imagine that things will be otherwise.

Frustration and irritation are close cousins of unpredictability. How short is your fuse? Studying overseas often requires a great deal of patience with people and situations that you would normally find intolerable in your own home environment. In the new environment where you are a foreigner, you are forced not only to tolerate, but also to accept. You would be ill-advised to think that everything will be just as you want it in your new environment overseas. The rules are not always the same as in your home country, and any attempt to make them so will be met with indifference or even hostility. Patience, tolerance and the ability to accept change are part of every overseas student's armour—those who not do possess these gifts in abundance should reconsider carefully.

CULTURE SHOCK

No careful approach to the possibility of living and working overseas—especially as a student—will be complete without at least some consideration of the culture shock phenomenon. Unlike a disease, culture shock is not selective and its onset is an inevitable part of moving from a known environment to an unknown one. Whether your overseas study might take you to Britain, Burma or Botswana, coping with culture shock—to whatever extent it may smite you—is undoubtedly going to be part of the experience.

Experts writing on the subject of culture shock have identified four distinct phases that anyone going to live abroad experiences. The length of each phase varies with the individual but, in general, each phase lasts longer than the preceding one. The four phases appear to be:

1) Fascination
An initial period when everything is new and there are seemingly few problems as everyone is being extremely accommodating. The predominant feeling at this time is one of exhilaration at being overseas at last after a long period of anticipation.

2) Friendship
Immediately following the initial euphoria comes the stage in which the need to structure a new social and support system to replace the one left behind becomes paramount. At this time, there is an understandable, but potentially unwise, tendency to befriend only those from your own country who are in a situation similar to yours, as a way of taking refuge in the familiar. This can easily develop into a "we-they" syndrome.

3) Frustration
After enough time has elapsed for you to familiarise yourself with the country, make initial contacts with the people and come to grips with the requirements of the new situation, a stage of depression begins when the problems and difficulties that are an inevitable part of the adjustment process seem to outweigh any possible, or potential, sense of achievement. This feeling is often heightened, unintentionally, when you get together with other overseas students and the conversation focuses on how much better things were back home.

There, in the new culture that you are learning to adapt to, the local people seem to have become intransigent, the physical environment unpleasant and the demands of others impossible to fulfil—with the result that hostility towards the host country and those who are in authority becomes the predominant emotion, and homesickness is the by-product. This frustration sometimes mounts to such a degree that there is a tendency (to which some people occasionally succumb) to decide that the whole experience is not worth it and that an early return home is preferable to remaining permanently miserable.

4) Fulfilment

Fortunately, although the previous stage can be a very difficult one to live through, it does usually come to an end as the cultural comfort level increases. This then leads to a period in which the experience of studying overseas becomes both fulfilling and rewarding. The onset of this phase stems from a personal realisation and acceptance that the new environment, in all its aspects, is unlikely to change and that, if the experience is to be satisfying, it is the individual who must adapt to the new environment by learning to operate within its confines. This may result in compromises but it will also bring about a realisation that conflicts can be worked out, and that the potential for success and happiness during the time spent abroad is as great as the individual is prepared to let it be.

When going to live in a new country, some degree of culture shock is bound to set in but there are ways to minimise its impact and shorten the stage when frustration and hostility set in. The first of these ways is to be aware of what is happening: to recognise the symptoms of culture shock as they occur and to share with others the feelings that each phase generates. This will help you to avoid the feeling of isolation which is so destructive in the long run. The second is to find new ways of coping with old (and new) problems, so that flexible thinking can lead to satisfactory resolutions instead of permanent inertia. Finally, and perhaps most important of all, it is imperative to set reasonable and achievable goals for the experience of studying wherever you are (even if these goals have to be modified from those you had hoped to achieve before leaving home). You will then have to find ways of achieving these goals, whether they be as simple as personal survival or as complex as complete cultural and linguistic understanding.

Deciding on whether you can survive the impact of culture shock, and the methods at your disposal for doing so, are important considerations in making the final decision to try the overseas experience. Preparing for its onslaught is half the battle won. How willing are you to learn a new language or adopt other ways of doing things, even if they may seem silly to you at first? Cultural frictions are going to be a big part of the experience you are considering and the success or failure of your overseas study experience may depend, to a large extent, not on how well you can retain your own cultural "baggage", or how successful you are in getting rid of it, but on how well you can integrate its best aspects with the best aspects of the new culture so that eventually, you can feel as equally at home in your new environment as you did in the one from which you came.

One other aspect of culture shock which you should also be careful not to ignore is the "reverse culture shock syndrome" that occurs when you return home. Many people who go overseas to work or study prepare themselves carefully and thoroughly for the impact of a new culture on their lives and habits but few of them give any thought to what will happen when they return home. Most work on the premise that things will be the same as when they left, so why bother?

This kind of thinking is a fallacy. Regardless of how long you have been away—whether one year or 10—things will not be exactly the same as they were before you left. Situations change, the people and environment you had left behind change—and all this happens gradually over a period of time during which you had relatively minimal contact with your home base. Perhaps the biggest change of all lies in yourself, although this is probably the hardest to recognise.

Living and working in a different way in a different environment, and following a different set of cultural rules, gradually alters your perspective on the way you do things and the way you expect others to relate to you.

> *"One of the biggest reverse culture shocks I had ever experienced was on my return from my first extended period of living overseas when, full of enthusiasm, I offered to give a talk to some of my friends on my experiences. I was devastated to find that the interest they had expressed in seeing my slides and hearing my comments was only a polite one, and that they really had no intrinsic interest in learning about all the new things that I had seen and done. I realised later that this wasn't really indifference, however, but simply an inability to understand and relate to the concepts and ideas that I was talking about because it was totally foreign to their own experience and they had no way of relating to it. So my stay overseas had changed me, but not them and, as a result, the relationship between us was subtly different from the one we had before I left."*
> —BB, a Canadian in Asia

Everybody who has lived overseas for a while and returns home faces this dilemma—and it applies to all relationships, be they with parents, children or friends. There is nothing that can be done to change this fact but, if you are prepared for it to happen and are not dismayed when it does, you can save yourself a lot of heartache and potentially difficult confrontations over changed relationships.

THE FINAL DECISION

Now, it is almost time to make the final decision and commit yourself to change! If you have read this far, you may feel that what is needed now is some way of deciding whether or not to proceed further, and start looking at the actual possibilities for studying overseas. So try the following self-preparedness survey and see how you rate.

There are three fundamentally important questions to be answered in making the decision to start looking:

1. Will I function well as a student overseas?
2. Will I enjoy the experience?
3. How am I actually going to try and find a place to study?

To get some idea of how you might answer these fundamental questions, the issues which they address have been divided into 20 smaller and more concrete areas. Try answering the smaller issues first, and then address the bigger ones. If you are totally honest with yourself, the more positive and optimistic your answers, the better you will probably be able to cope overseas. But beware! The penalty for cheating on yourself may well be an ignominious failure rather than a well-deserved success. (It may be a good idea to have your spouse or best friend rate you as well, and compare the answers!)

Leaving home

1. What emotional ties do I have at home? Can I deal with them at a distance?
2. What practical commitments do I have at home? Can they be satisfactorily dealt with by others in my absence?
3. How will I react to living in another country in which the customs and traditions are different from those I am used to?
4. Will I feel cut off if I am not involved in what goes on around me the same way that I am at home?
5. How well will I cope with homesickness and loneliness?
6. How well will I be able to readjust when I return and resume my life at home?

Considering the options

7. How do I feel about leaving what I am doing presently? What avenues are open to me to go abroad to study?
8. What kind of school abroad can I get into? Is this the kind of studying experience I really want?
9. How easy is it for me to adapt my skills and studying strategies to different requirements?
10. How well do I cope with frustration or failure?
11. How important is it to me that I should feel comfortable in a familiar school environment?
12. How willing am I to live on a strange campus?

Adapting to another culture

13. How will I react to being suddenly cut off from things that I enjoy doing?
14. How easy is it for me to establish new relationships with people?
15. Do I have any prejudices? How will they affect my attitude towards others?
16. How important to me is my personal freedom to do what I want? Can I survive curtailment of this freedom, and to what degree?
17. How much privacy do I need? Can I survive with very little?
18. How important are my material possessions? Can I do without most of them for a time?

General decisions

19. How well do I know myself? What I am *really* like?
20. How willing am I to venture somewhat blindly into the unknown?

Chapter Two

THE RIGHT PLACE

☛ *In the next few chapters, you may come across some terms commonly used by universities and colleges, but with which you may not be familiar yet. Many of these terms are explained in Part One of the Appendix found at the end of this book.*

The decision to spend a part of your life studying in another country, living and working with people you have never met, is not one to be taken lightly. Long before you set foot on the aeroplane and wave goodbye to weeping family and friends, there is a great deal to find out about and many crucial decisions to be made.

One of best ways of ensuring that you get all the facts you

need to make the most appropriate decisions is to do a very thorough job of researching what your alternatives are and which of them are most suited to your personal circumstances. This section takes you through the research process and suggests several things you need to consider before you take any positive action to apply for overseas studies.

CHOOSING YOUR COUNTRY OF STUDY

For most students, just thinking about studying overseas automatically creates visions of life as a student in one of the North American Ivy League colleges (Harvard, Princeton, Yale and so on) or in the hallowed halls of Oxford, Cambridge, Heidelburg or the Sorbonne. For some people, these dreams will be realised but the fact is that those who get to study in these prestigious institutions are more the exception than the rule. They will have either the kind of outstanding academic ability which will win them a scholarship to these places, or access to the vast sums of money that can sometimes serve as an alternative.

For the vast majority of those who are looking for opportunities to study overseas, the goals have to be more modest. Fortunately, there are several universities and colleges throughout the world which understand the value of having foreign students on their campuses, and the admission process for a student applying from overseas is as uncomplicated and fair as possible.

The crux of the matter, as anyone who has been through the process will tell you, is in finding the right place to apply to. Basically, it should be in a country where:

1. You speak the language relatively fluently,
2. The fees and overall costs of post-secondary study are manageable and within the budget you can afford.
3. You can obtain a student visa.

Without any one of these, studying overseas can almost become an impossible dream. The first step, then, is to determine the country in which you most want to study. The first and most important factor here is, of course, that of language—it is no use applying to any university where the language of instruction is one with which you are totally unfamiliar. It is a fallacy to think that this is unimportant and that you can pick up the language as you go along. The level of study at university requires a similar level of language skill, and you are just not going to have the time to master a new language and make good progress in your studies at the same time. So think carefully about your language skills before considering a country where the medium of instruction is not English, unless you are fluent in that country's language as well.

If this is not the case, you must be prepared to spend at least six months to a year attending language classes before you can begin to embark on your intended course of study.

> *"I decided to go to Japan because I was already studying the language in college ... but nevertheless, it was frustrating. Even after having taken a year of Japanese at Stanford, I was by no means prepared for the speed at which people actually spoke the language, and the grammar used was much more informal than what was taught in class."—YP, an American in Japan*

For a large number of countries, of course, language is not an issue. After all, English is the language of instruction in institutions in well over 30 countries. Britain, North America, Australia and New Zealand tend to be the top choices in this category and certainly, there is a tremendous range of possibilities, especially in the United States. However, school fees and costs vary widely for post-secondary programmes and this becomes another important factor in deciding which country to study in.

☛ *Establish at an early stage what you and your parents can afford to pay annually for your overseas studies, then use this amount to help you make a practical choice of which country to study in, not only in terms of the actual cost of education (more on this can be found in Chapter Four), but also the cost of expense items such as accommodation, food and transport. Nothing is more distressing to a student than running out of money during the academic year and having no way of getting any more!*

Another factor to consider in your choice of a country is how easy it is for you to get a visa to study there. In nearly every instance (with some exceptions for those students who are lucky enough to have some kind of dual citizenship), you will have to apply for a visa to study in the country of your choice—and the granting of this visa is not always automatic once you have been accepted by the institution you want to study in. There have been a number of unfortunate incidents in the past when students have been accepted into overseas institutions, completed the paperwork, paid all the fees, and then found that they could not get a visa for some reason! Happily, however, this situation is the exception rather than the rule.

☞ *In most cases, a visa will be granted once admission into a university has been confirmed, but it is still wise to check with the embassy of the country concerned before you begin the actual application process. This is to save yourself from running into problems later.*

If you can speak the language, have the money and can get the visa, then the world is your oyster and you can begin to choose your country and move on to the next step of researching for the specific institution and programme that you want. One final word of advice, though, especially if you are looking at a professional programme. Make sure that the qualifications that you will receive overseas are recognised and accepted in your own country when you return!

CHOOSING YOUR INSTITUTION

There are two very important criteria to consider in making this decision. Firstly, make sure that you choose an institution which has a programme that caters to what you hope to achieve by studying overseas and secondly, that the qualifications you already have meet with its admission requirements.

Before you set out to do this, however, the most important thing to note is that the terminology used to describe post-secondary institutions around the world is by no means uniform. Basically, a university is always a university but a college is not always a university as well. A polytechnic can be an university but this is not always so!

To sort out the confusion, it is very important to make a distinction—that between a degree, and a diploma or certificate. A degree is a qualification which almost always refers to the outcome of an university education, and is usually described as a Bachelor's degree (the first degree awarded to a fresh graduate) or Master's degree (one of the graduate degrees awarded after completion of the first degree). Some American universities also award an Associate degree which is also a first degree, but as these degrees usually represent less than three years of university study, they are not widely recognised outside the United States. Many universities also award Master's degrees and Doctoral degrees but these are not achieved by the majority of university students as they require at least four or five years, or previous university study, before they can even be embarked upon.

☛ *If you are looking for an undergraduate university education, make sure that you will receive a Bachelor's degree (or its equivalent) at the conclusion of the course of study you are planning to take. If your planned study is at the graduate level, make sure that you have the first degree qualifications to apply for it and that it will lead to either a Master's degree or a Doctoral degree.*

If taking a particular course of study is more important than achieving a degree for it, then you might want to broaden your search to include colleges that issue diplomas, as opposed to restricting yourself to universities. But be careful, especially when looking towards the United States, as the term "college" there usually refers to the same kind of institution as does the term "university"—although not all the time. There may be further confusion for foreign students when some universities operate what they call a "college system" in which the main university is divided internally into a number of smaller, semi-autonomous units known as colleges, each with its own identity.

Outside the United States, however, it is usually understood that at a college, the qualification you obtain is called either a diploma or a certificate, representing more the completion of a specific course of study and your proficiency in that area than graduation from the more general type of educational experience offered at university.

Perhaps this difference can best be illustrated by looking at the differences in function between a university and college. Put very simply, the basic function of most programmes at university is to train the brain in higher thinking skills so that the student is able to solve problems in his or her chosen discipline at a complex level. The basic function of a college programme, on the other hand, is to train the hands of the student to perform a specific task at a sophisticated level. For instance, a university graduate with a degree in civil engineering should have the skills to plan, design and work out the problems associated with building a particular bridge, while the construction foreman who interprets this design and actually works on building the bridge might be a college graduate with a diploma in construction engineering technology. Polytechnics and polytechnical institutes are similar to colleges in this way, and produce the same kind of graduates.

This does not mean that colleges and their diploma programmes are inferior to those offered at universities (although there is a social tendency in some countries to believe that they are). Instead, they exist to serve a different purpose.

☛ *In choosing whether to attend a university or college overseas, it is important to check carefully what kind of qualification the institution grants and what that certification will mean to you in terms of securing a job when you return to your home country.*

If you are satisfied that the kind of institution you want to study in overseas meets the needs that you have determined, then include as wide a range of places as possible and then narrow your choice according to the actual content of the programmes each offers, its reputation in its own country and in yours, the suitability of its location and the cost of the education that it provides.

CHOOSING YOUR PROGRAMME OF STUDY

The programme you choose will, of course, depend largely on what you are interested in studying and the reason for your wanting to study it. Firstly, make sure that you have noted the caution in the preceding section—there is no point in going overseas to study if the qualification you receive at the end of it is of no use in the country you will return home to.

With this in mind, your research should lead you to publications such as the *International Handbook of Universities*, which will tell you which universities exist in each country and what areas of study they provide. This publication and other useful sources of information are listed in the Appendix at the back of this book. The rest is relatively easy: a letter to the university of your choice should get you a copy of its current calendar. This will have a detailed listing of all its programmes, as well as the entry requirements for them.

If you have a country in mind, a visit to that country's representative office—the embassy or consulate—will be a trip worth making. Most embassies have a wide selection of calendars from post-secondary institutions in their own country that you can browse through. There may even be an embassy official, such as a student adviser, who can give you the general information you require—the cost of studying overseas, and visa and health requirements, for example.

Most countries have universities which provide programmes in the main areas of study such as engineering, medicine, law, education, psychology, nursing and fine arts, although not all programmes are necessarily offered at all universities. In fact, some countries even have specialist universities which concentrate on only one area of study.

Be aware also in your programme research that in some countries, some disciplines are offered as first-degree programmes whereas, in other countries, you may need to be in possession of a degree already in order to access the same programme. Professional disciplines such as medicine and law are good examples of this type of programme. You should also consider the fact that if you already have some university credits from your home country, they may not be accepted on par at the university you are applying to and you may have to repeat some of these courses at that university before it will admit you to the course of your choice.

> "My decision to study abroad was influenced by two factors. Firstly, psychology, which was my area of interest, was not established in Singapore and secondly, I was lucky enough to be given the option by my family to study abroad. I chose to study in Canada as it was financially affordable and I had relatives close by. I had to go through college first to gain enough credits to enter university. My choice of Canadian college and university was decided upon after I had gone through adver-

tisements in the local newspaper, had consultations with Canadian embassy personnel in Singapore and attended talks by the Singapore representative of the Canadian college."—BR, a Singaporean in Canada

FINDING THE RIGHT ADMISSION ROUTE
A) Through the major national systems

The problem with national educational systems worldwide is that they are not in any way uniform. What is required for secondary school graduation in one country may not even resemble the qualifications required for the same thing in another. This leads to problems such as those discussed in the previous section where, although you may possess adequate qualifications for admission to a university in your home country, these may not be acceptable in the country you are planning to study in.

There is no easy way to determine your acceptability in one country based on qualifications from another—the easiest way to go about the matter is to send your secondary school (or univer-

sity) record to the institution you want to attend and ask it to assess your qualifications for admission to your chosen programme. The university will then be able to tell you whether you can apply right away or if you need to meet further criteria for admission to the course of study you want. Sometimes, the embassies or high commissions can help you with this too but you will usually have to approach the institution directly. Also, if the educational system you are currently enrolled in offers advanced courses of any kind, it is usually a good idea to complete them first as they may be of assistance to you when you choose to apply overseas.

B) By using international criteria

Probably one of the best ways to enhance your chances of gaining admission into the overseas university that you are eyeing is to acquire an internationally recognised qualification that is accepted at most post-secondary institutions worldwide.

The most well-known of these qualifications are probably the SAT and TOEFL examinations, required of all applicants to American universities and used by a good number of universities in other countries for admission purposes as well. The SAT (Scholastic Aptitude Test) is administered by the College Board of the United States and is available in two parts: a reasoning test (SAT 1) and subject specific tests (SAT 2). You will usually be required to write the SAT 1, which consists of two main sections—one verbal and one mathematical—and, depending on the university to which you are applying, you may also be asked to write one of the subjects covered by the SAT 2 tests. Both SATs must be taken at a recognised centre (of which there are many all over the world) on one of the dates preset by the SAT administrators. Universities which require the SAT will indicate this when they send you admission materials and, if you want to find out more about it, you can always ask the United States Information Service (USIS) in the country in which you live, or you can write directly to the College Board at Suite 250, 2970 Clairmont Road, Atlanta, Georgia, USA 30329-1634.

Occasionally, universities will ask you to take the ACT (American College Test) instead of the SAT as part of the admission process. This is another universally recognised College Entrance Assessment Test, developed and administered by the University of Iowa. It is very similar to SAT, having sections dealing with English, mathematics, reading and scientific reasoning. As in the case of the SAT, ACT can be prepared for by reading up on commercial publications that explain in detail the kinds of questions the test contains, giving suggestions on how you can perform well if you are asked to take this test instead of the SAT. Further information about the ACT can be obtained from the American College Testing Program, PO Box 168, Iowa City, Iowa, USA 52243.

The TOEFL (Test of English as a Foreign Language), along with its companion tests, the TWE (Test of Written English) and TSE (Test of Spoken English), is administered by the Educational Testing Service at Rosedale Road, Princeton, New Jersey, USA 08541, and can also be taken worldwide. This proficiency test in English is usually required of all non-native speakers of English applying to a university in an English-speaking country. It consists of three sections: listening comprehension, structure and written expression, and vocabulary and reading comprehension. Calendars from the individual university you are interested in will usually indicate whether you need to take the TOEFL as part of the application process.

Sometimes, specific universities have their own English-language examinations, similar to the TOEFL, that they may require you to take, either in addition to the TOEFL or, at times, instead of the TOEFL. There are also a couple of other standardised tests of English-language proficiency you may encounter: the Short Selection Test (SST) that the Australian Department of Employment, Education and Training uses, and the International English Language Testing System (IELTS), a joint British-Australian test.

If you are applying for postgraduate study, you may also be required to take the Graduate Management Admission Test (GMAT) or the Graduate Record Examination (GRE). For admission to professional courses of study, the Medical College Admissions Test (MCAT) and the Law School Admission Test (LSAT) are also widely used.

There is another international university entrance qualification which has been growing in popularity over the past 10 years or so, and is now much more widely available then it used to be. This is the International Baccalaureate (IB) examination which is offered as part of the senior school curriculum in many schools all over the world. It is a difficult examination and requires two years of preparatory study to take. The curriculum is divided into six subjects: your native language, a foreign language (one of which should usually be English), mathematics, science, a social science and one other subject of your choice. In addition to this, the diploma also requires the completion of an extended essay on a topic related to one of your areas of study, completion of a course in the theory of knowledge, as well as a predetermined number of hours of community service. Many universities worldwide accept this credential for entry to undergraduate study and can give you information on what they specifically require, if you have access to a school that offers this programme.

C) By using international placement agencies or other educational services

If you do not feel comfortable approaching universities yourself or find the task too daunting to tackle on your own, most countries have agencies which will help you in your search. Some of these agencies (such as the Malaysian-American Centre for Education Exchange, or MACEE, in Kuala Lumpur, Malaysia) are run by the government of the country you want to study in and do not charge for the information you need or the help that they can give you with the application process.

However, there are other private agencies that are run for profit by people who are familiar with the post-secondary system in the country you want to go to. These agencies will charge a fee for the information and help that they are able to give you. Some of these agencies are reputable and can be useful in helping you to narrow down your choices and in determining whether you have the qualifications to do what you want. But there are a few places where the information can be dubious and overpriced, so you should exercise caution in choosing this method of application. Always double-check the information you receive with the university itself before you go too far with the process or pay large sums of money for it.

☛ *It is worth remembering that these agencies can only help but cannot secure direct admission for you, even if they say they can. Make sure that you check exactly what the relationship of the agency is with the universities and colleges it is supposed to represent because it is very easy for you to be misled, especially when you are not familiar with the application process.*

For the same reason, beware also of travelling agents who may arrive in your country and promise easy admission to specific universities if you pay them a sum of money. At best, these agents have been authorised by the university to screen potential applications and then refer any promising possibilities to it for a final decision. At worst, these agents can be charlatans who have no more direct connections with any university than you could have had yourself if you were simply to write it a letter.

If you can—even though it may take longer and involve a little more work—it is best to handle the university admission process yourself, with some guidance from a government-sponsored agency, if one exists.

D) Through secondary study in a school overseas

This is often a good option, but is usually expensive. There are two ways of acquiring a foreign secondary school qualification: one is to attend an international school in the country in which you live, and the other is to travel to the country you want to study in and enrol in a secondary school there which offers the credential you need.

Such schools are usually private ones, however, and they charge sizeable fees as the national systems will not usually admit students who are just visitors to the country and who have not immigrated there.

If you choose to study locally in an international school, it is preferable to select one which offers the International Baccalaureate as its graduation diploma as this will make it easier for you to get into a university overseas. You will also usually need a good academic track record as many international schools are selective about whom they enrol. Also, you can expect to pay anything from US$5,000 to US$15,000 a year to attend such a school.

Studying overseas at the secondary level will usually require that a student visa be obtained for the country you wish to study in and, as has been pointed out earlier, this can sometimes be a problem, even if you have already been accepted by the school.

Sometimes, you will need a sponsor in that country who can guarantee that you have enough money to complete your studies there. In addition, proof is sometimes required that you have access to enough cash yourself to complete your intended programme of study before you are granted a visa. Note also that the granting of a visa for secondary study overseas does not necessarily mean that you will automatically be granted the same visa for continuing at university level.

However, if you can afford to pay the fees and are eligible for a visa, you will usually find plenty of schools in the country of your choice that can provide you with a suitable course of study.

☞   *Be a little careful in your choice as not all private schools provide the same quality of education. If you are in doubt, check with the embassy or consulate or, better still, consult someone who has studied in that country.*

E) Through a student exchange

Student exchanges are usually a good way to check out a country you may want to study in later or, if you are already in university, to study the possibilities of future employment. But they are not usually a good way to get a credential which will be helpful in gaining admission to a post-secondary institution.

The reason is simple—exchanges are usually too short to complete a useful programme of study. Most student exchange programmes take place during the third or fourth year of a student's undergraduate course of study and are designed to achieve a specific purpose, such as enabling a student of political science to study first-hand the political system of another country. Such programmes cannot, however, be used as a way of entering a specific institution for the purpose of obtaining a degree. This is because the course work which is done is always related to a particular field of study at the university from which the exchange student comes.

Nevertheless, exchange programmes are quite common at universities all over the world and can provide a useful short-term study exposure abroad if it is the experience itself and not the qualification which is being sought.

THE BONUSES OF GRADUATE STUDY

As a graduate student studying abroad, you will have certain advantages that are not available to the undergraduate student. Not the least of these is the way in which the university and its faculty will treat you and the studies you are undertaking.

Graduate students from overseas usually find that their relationship with their fellow students and professors is much more of a relationship between colleagues compared to what it was like at the undergraduate level. Studying overseas at the graduate level is a much more established practice than at the undergraduate level and, provided that your undergraduate degree is a good one, you should find much less trouble in getting your entry qualifications evaluated and being accepted into the programme of your choice than would an undergraduate student.

Visas, too, are often more readily given for the purpose of undertaking studies at the graduate level than they are at the undergraduate level. This is particularly so in the case of students who come from countries where there may be some kind of quota system—imposed by the host country—for the granting of student visas to those originating from those countries.

There are also increased opportunities for graduate students to work on the university campus. Many universities employ graduate students as part-time teaching assistants in the department in which their own courses are being offered and these jobs often come with a reasonable salary. The work usually entails tutoring and guiding undergraduate students and sometimes marking their work—chores which do not take a great deal of time so that there is still enough time for your own studies.

If you cannot find work as a teaching assistant, the university libraries and other internal departments often use graduate students as part-time employees, so the opportunity to finance a sizeable part of your education overseas is available in a way that it is not to an undergraduate. Similarly, there are often more avenues and opportunities to secure scholarship and bursary money for the overseas graduate student then for an undergraduate student.

Postponing overseas studies until the graduate level can be a very good option for a student whose financial resources are limited, but whose academic skills have been well demonstrated to be superior during his or her undergraduate years. The comparatively simpler admission process, the greater availability of financial assistance and the way in which graduate students are regarded by their university colleagues all make overseas study at this level very attractive.

SOURCES FOR RESEARCH

There are at least five ways in which you can do most of the research described in this chapter—the most useful one, unfortunately, being the least accessible to the student applying from abroad.

A) Visiting the university or post-secondary institution

Making a personal visit is by far the best way to learn much about a place in a short time. Most institutions are delighted to host prospective students and will set up a visit following a letter or phone call. If you can, try and visit personally at least some of the institutions that you are interested in—there is no other way to get a flavour of the place.

B) Talking to graduates of a particular university

This is often possible to arrange in one of two ways—by meeting with graduates of an institution who happen to live in your country or by attending a meeting held by visiting university representatives. When you write to the institutions that you are interested in, ask them for a list of their graduates who live in your country, or if any of their representatives will be visiting your country in the near future. Most places will be delighted to give you this information—and it can be very useful if you have a lot of questions to which you are looking for answers.

C) Writing to the institutions

This is something which anyone who is considering studying overseas should do as a matter of course. Most post-secondary institutions are only too happy to send out materials about themselves to people who take the trouble to write to them.

Usually, the only cost for this is that of the postage stamp to despatch your letter there, although some universities now charge for their catalogues to keep their costs down and make sure that they are sent only to serious enquirers.

D) Using audio-visual and computer materials

Several institutions will send out videos, either free or for a nominal charge, to prospective applicants and, if you cannot actually get there, this is the next best way of seeing what a particular place is like. Information on colleges is sometimes available on computer disk too, so ask about this when you write.

E) Written materials

A wide range of materials is available on studying abroad in general and on the university and college systems in various countries. Many of these are listed in the Bibliography at the end of this book and you would do well to look at those that appear most relevant to you before you start writing letters. The answers to many of your initial questions may be in there!

Chapter Three

THE APPLICATION PROCESS

HE'S APPLYING TO AN AUSTRALIAN COLLEGE

The university academic year varies in different parts of the world so you, as an aspiring student, will have to look at the calendar to see where you fit in.

UNDERSTANDING THE ACADEMIC YEAR

In most Northern Hemisphere countries, the post-secondary school year follows a similar pattern. Students begin their studies in the early part of September—in the United States, traditionally the day after Labour Day, which is the first Monday in September—after completing a registration process.

For first-year students, the date of arrival at the university may have to be a little earlier than that of the upperclassmen (undergraduate students not in their first year). This is partly because it often takes longer to register due to unfamiliarity with the expected course structure, and partly because of the special events that are organised specifically for the freshmen (first-year undergraduate students) to orientate them to their new surroundings and provide a vehicle for introduction to other students new to the institution.

Classes generally begin within a week of arrival at the institution and continue without a break until just before the Christmas period, when the examinations for the first term are held. Students return in early January and begin their classes for the second term, which run until late April. There is often a one-week break during this second term, which occurs in February and is known (often rather ironically) as reading week. During this week, all classes are suspended and the students are free to follow their own conscience as to how they will use the time. Some students do spend the time studying but a far larger number use the week as a holiday, travelling to their homes or going with groups of other students to traditional holiday locations for a week of relaxation.

Examinations for the second term are held through April and students traditionally leave the university for their four-month summer vacation at the end of this month. Many students take jobs during the summer months to help offset the cost of their course of study and such jobs traditionally start towards the end of May and run until the end of August.

Of course, many post-secondary institutions in the Southern Hemisphere have an academic year which does not follow this pattern, traditionally starting some time in January or early February and ending late in the year, usually around the end of October or November. Still other systems, such as that in Japan and other countries in which major holidays other than the Christian ones are observed, have different starting dates for their academic year, so it is always wise to check with someone connected with the country you intend to study in to find out exactly when the school year begins. Unfortunately, the different starting dates sometimes create a problem for international students—when they try to time the start of their post-secondary studies right after the end of their secondary ones—but there is usually little that can be done to avoid this.

THE APPLICATION PROCESS EXPLAINED

The first and most fundamental point to note about applying to post-secondary institutions overseas is that there is no standardisation of the process. Sometimes, there is a national processing centre that can be used for university applications to one particular country (such as the Universities Central Council on Admissions, or UCCA, in the United Kingdom) or a regional one for one particular area of a country (such as the Ontario Universities Application Centre, or OUAC, in Ontario, Canada). More often than not, however, application has to be made directly to the university concerned. This means that the prospective student has to gather together and wade through a sizeable number of application materials, often with different deadlines for submission and all involving payment of an application or processing fee.

☛ *There is no short-cut method of getting around the mechanics of this process, but this is where the agencies referred to in the previous chapter can sometimes be the most helpful. Without cost, they should, at least, tell you when the academic year begins and give you access to a list of the post-secondary institutions in the country or countries with which they deal, and then leave it up to you to get in contact with those that interest you. If an agency does more than this—advise you on a specific choice and help you with the admission process itself, for example—it will very often charge for its services but, depending on the reputation of the agency and how much it charges, it is often worthwhile to accept this help as it can save you a lot of time in the long run.*

Once you have chosen your country or countries, selected the institutions that interest you, determined as accurately as you can that you are eligible to apply for the programme you want and gathered the necessary application materials, you are ready to begin!

Bearing in mind the cost of the application process and the time it will take, it is essential to make sure that you have enough time to complete everything by the deadlines given by the individual universities for international students. Then determine how many of the post-secondary institutions you are actually going to apply to.

At this stage, you may want to opt for the "shotgun approach" in which you gather information on a range of institutions, either one or two in each of the countries you are interested in, or several in the one country that you have targeted. In your preliminary research, you should also get some sense of the degree of competition for places at each of the institutions you target. What you should do is to try and make sure that, among your choices, there are some to which you would like to be admitted, but for which you think that the competition might be stiff; some to which you should get admitted unless there is some unusually heavy competition in the year that you apply; and others to which you ought to be admitted under any circumstances.

Then there is the application process itself. Universities worldwide are usually interested in three types of information about you:

- Who you are and what your academic track record is like.
- What other people in your life think about you both as a scholar and human being.
- What you think about yourself.

The first type of information is usually gathered by means of an application form which asks for personal information (such as name, address, nationality and sex) and your academic track record, which normally has to be supported by documentation such as a transcript (containing a complete record of the marks obtained in all the courses that you have taken) sent directly to the institution by the school you currently attend or last went to.

The second type of information can be gathered in a number of ways, but the most common is in the form of references written by those people who know you best in the various areas of your life. This can be one or two of your former teachers, your guidance counsellor or school principal, or sometimes friends of the family who have known you for many years. These references, when they are required, are usually submitted directly by your referees to the institution.

The third type of information is usually the most difficult to supply and it can take many forms. Universities in the United States, for instance, will often ask you to write a personal essay—

sometimes a very challenging thing to do as it is very difficult to write about yourself in a way which gives a total stranger a sense of your positive qualities and personality traits without sounding immodest or stilted.

The important thing in writing such as essay is to forget what you think they want to hear and just be natural in what you say. If you can put a little of yourself and a sense of the place you live in into these essays, you will not go far wrong. Universities other than those in the United States will try and elicit this information in other ways—through supplementary application forms and aptitude tests, for example—but the bottom line is that they want to know what kind of person you are outside the classroom and how well you will fit in to their institution if they were to admit you.

There are two other possible components of an application package which you may be asked to provide. The first of these is a statement of financial support in which you or your parents (or other financial backers) must state the source and nature of the funds that are intended to support you through university. This is usually calculated before you receive any kind of external financial aid and it has to, at least, appear sufficiently close to what it will cost you to attend the place you have in mind before the rest of your application can be considered. (See the next chapter for further information about finances.)

The other part of the process can be submission of your standardised test scores, such as the SAT and TOEFL discussed in the last chapter. You may be asked to put these on your application form if they are required but, as part of the testing process, they are usually also submitted directly to the universities you name as part of the reporting process. Make sure that you take the required standardised tests well in advance of your actual application deadline as it takes time to apply, sit for the tests and get the results, and the absence of score information on the tests can delay the whole admission process for you.

THE STUDY SCHEDULE

If you intend to study overseas, it is a good idea to regard the whole process as a two-year project starting 24 months before the date that you want to start studying. Here is a suggested time frame that should serve as a guide:

The first year

1. Conduct your own research in large public and local university libraries to find out what countries you would like to study in, and which universities there offer the programmes you want to take.

2. Visit the embassies and consulates of the countries you are interested in, both to look at any university calendars that they may have on post-secondary opportunities and to confirm that you will be able to get a student visa to study there if you are accepted by one of their institutions.

3. Send letters directly to the universities or colleges you are interested in, asking them to send you a calendar, information on the admission process, details of any financial assistance scheme they may have (for example, scholarships) if you think you will need this, and any other information that is relevant to someone applying from your country. (See Part Two of the Appendix for a sample letter.)

4. Talk to any graduates of universities overseas and ask about their experiences and whether they have any advice that would be useful for what you are planning to do. (When you write to the universities, you can ask them to send you the names and addresses of any graduates that they may have living in your country. Most of them will be happy to accede to your request.)

5. Make a preliminary list of institutions you have gathered information about and put them in a priority order for application purposes. Review this information carefully and make sure that you have all the materials you need in order

to begin the actual application process.

6. Consider taking any tests which are going to be part of the application process (for example, SAT or TOEFL). If you do not perform very well the first time, it will be good practice at least and you can always take the test again the following year.

7. Consider who you are going to ask to write recommendations for you if these are needed, and inform the people concerned that you will be asking for their testimonials early in the following year, so that they have some time to think of what they are going to say about you.

8. If you are able to, make arrangements to visit the country you want to study in (perhaps with your parents or a friend, if possible) and, while there, try and visit one or two of the university campuses that you are interested in. Most universities will set up tours and appointments for you to talk to faculty members if you notify them in advance of the date of your visit.

9. Make a personal calendar listing important dates and deadlines which you must adhere to during the following year.

10. Take a deep breath and enjoy a break for the holidays!

The Second Year

1. Register early for any tests you need to take but have not taken yet (SAT 1 and 2, TOEFL, ACT, GRE, and so on) and start reviewing what you will need to know for them. (There are lots of books you can buy which will help you with this, and most of them contain sample test materials). Make sure that, upon your application, you indicate the places to which you want copies of your scores sent, since most testing agencies send the scores directly to the institution at the same time that they report them to you.

2. Review your school or other academic transcript with a qualified counsellor (at your school or at a recognised agency)

to confirm that you are eligible for admission to wherever it is you want to go—either at the present time or by the time you are ready to start.

3. Finalise and prioritise your top choices for application—by this stage, you should probably have no more than 10 or so—or the whole process will become rather unwieldy and somewhat expensive. Make sure that you are familiar with the admission process for these places and that you have the necessary application forms. (If you do not, write immediately to the institutions to get them.)

4. Start to fill out and submit your applications. Keep copies of everything you send and take note of the dates on which they are despatched. (If you are in any doubt about your postal service, send them by some form of delivery where their receipt will have to be acknowledged.) Make sure that appropriate processing fees are enclosed, and in the currency in which the institution has requested them to be sent.

5. Ensure that you have given everyone who has to write a report on you, or who is responsible for submitting your academic transcript, the appropriate forms. Check too that they are well aware of the way in which they are supposed to submit the forms (either directly to the institution concerned or by returning them to you) and the deadline by which these have to be received by the other party.

6. If necessary, make sure that you have gathered the necessary financial guarantee forms so that you will be able to prove that you have sufficient funds to travel to, study in and return home from the country and institution you are planning to go to. This may be required by the university or for the purpose of obtaining a student visa.

7. If you have determined that you are eligible for financial assistance, complete and mail out any financial aid forms that you may have been given, or complete the application

process for any scholarships and/or bursaries for which you qualify. (See the next chapter for more information on this.)

8. Wait—holding your breath!—for replies from the institutions you have applied to. These should probably arrive any time between two and six months prior to the date you intend to start. On arrival, celebrate if appropriate—but do not forget to check what financial deposits you have to pay to keep your place!

9. With your acceptance in hand, go to the appropriate embassy or consulate to apply for your student visa. Make sure that you leave enough time for this to be processed, as it can take up to two months and, in most cases, you will not be allowed to travel to the country you are going to until your visa is ready—even if the term has started!

10. Say goodbye—and off you go!

HOW UNIVERSITIES DECIDE

Because the application process itself is not standardised, basically there are as many ways in which decisions are made as there are universities all over the world to make them. However, there are a few general guidelines which, while not infallible, will at least give you some idea of what chance you stand of getting admitted.

Academically, it is important that your school record to date be consistent, especially if you are applying to very competitive places. The Dean of Admissions at Amherst College, one of the United States' most competitive universities, is quoted as saying that "the quality of a student's academic programme—throughout secondary school—will continue to be the first thing we look at when we read through an application." If your marks in your senior years of secondary schooling are lower than those in your ninth or 10th years, then post-secondary institutions are often more likely not to consider you a serious academic student.

Going along with this is the fact that the more competitive

the institution, the more likely it is to pay greater attention to the more subjective attributes of its applicants. Many of these very competitive places (and not only the likes of Harvard, Princeton, Oxford or the Sorbonne) receive applications from several hundred more really well qualified people than they can possibly admit in a given year, so this is when other criteria such as recommendations, documented personal achievements and written submissions, such as personal essays, will assume great importance.

Obviously, this means that admission to these places is less predictable than it would be to a college which is only concerned that you have the required academic standing. In systems that are geared more exclusively towards examination results (Japan, for example), this can cause some anxiety and even concern. Who knows if Princeton may need a viola player for its orchestra

this year? Or if several members of a top-rated swimming team have recently graduated from Oxford? When so many applicants have outstanding academic records, little factors such the ability to play an instrument or to swim competitively can make a big difference. Unfortunately, individual applicants have little control over this, but it does underscore the need to be an all-round student when applying to very competitive places—and to make sure that the universities are aware of your skills well in advance.

In universities where standardised test scores are required, they can assume quite a bit of importance, particularly as far as language skills and background in the subject area you plan to study in are concerned. The TOEFL test is one where your scores should be as high as you can possibly make them (550 is usually the minimum considered as a sufficient level of language with which to undertake university study). If you are asked to take the SAT 2 achievement tests, English composition, mathematics, science, a foreign language and history are the most commonly requested subjects. You should probably score at least 500 in the subject area you are interested in if you are to appear at least competent.

After these criteria (academic standing, personal achievements, extracurricular activities and test scores) have been considered, a number of other small—and sometime intangible—criteria can also make a difference to whether you gain admittance or not.

☛ *The neatness and overall presentation of your application documents can make a difference in some places—so make sure that they are as flawless as you can make them and, if you can, type them out unless you have copper-plate handwriting! Your personal character and attributes can also count. This is a very hard thing for a university to gauge, but some will try to learn more about you through "reading between the lines" of your application and the recommendations submitted on your behalf.*

Universities are looking for evidence of integrity, thoughtfulness, creativity and self-confidence—all of which are characteristics that they believe will stand you in good stead at an overseas university. This comes through in what is said about what you have done and your attitude towards it—if you have been actively involved in many areas and have assumed leadership roles in some of them, you will be a far stronger candidate than if you had your nose stuck in your books for the whole of the preceding time.

There is also the question of your ability to pay the university fees. If you have all the money you need at home, and can prove this to the institution's satisfaction, so much the better. But if you are obviously going to need some financial help from somewhere, then money can become a factor in the admission process. Some institutions, especially in the United States, profess to be "need-blind" (meaning that the financial circumstances of the applicant have no bearing on whether or not he or she will be admitted. For those which are not "need blind"—and this refers to the majority of universities worldwide—your financial circumstances may be a factor in determining if you secure a place, whether this is morally right or not. Realistically, at most universities today, the people in charge of admissions have to limit the number of students they admit who will require some form of financial aid (this does not necessarily include scholarships that you may have been awarded). If you obviously cannot pay the course fees without some help, this fact can adversely affect your chances of admission. (See the next chapter for further information.)

A final word on trends—institutions which are perceived as currently "hot" places to go and study in can be harder to get into. Do not worry if they turn you down—there are usually plenty of other places just as good which have not been discovered yet!

THE ALL-IMPORTANT STUDENT VISA

Although regulations on the issuing of student visas vary from country to country, there are once again some general principles which will be applied in determining your eligibility for one.

1. Do you have a valid passport?
2. Have you submitted a fully and accurately completed application of which you have kept a copy?
3. Do you have a letter of acceptance (and other documentation if it has been supplied) from a recognised post-secondary institution for an approved course of study in that country to which you are applying for a student visa?
4. Can you demonstrate that sufficient financial support is available to you to cover the full cost of your course of study?
5. Are you prepared to give some form of guarantee that you will leave that country as soon as your studies are completed?

If the answer to any of these questions is "no", then you will probably not be eligible for a student visa. If you meet all these provisions, then check with the embassy or consulate to make sure that there is no further information that they require of you before you put in your application. Properly completed documentation and an obviously well-organised approach to the whole process of studying abroad will cause the process to proceed much faster than it might otherwise. If you can, give yourself an allowance of several weeks between your application for a visa and the time you actually want to leave—it will make you a lot more comfortable when planning for your departure if you know that the visa is on its way!

Chapter Four

FINDING THE FUNDING

There are some general rules of thumb which you must consider when calculating the cost of studying abroad but, as the cost varies so greatly from country to country and from institution to institution, there can be no specific guidelines that apply to all situations.

DETERMINING THE COST

Generally, the following lists the main costs of studying overseas which you will have to budget for. More detailed information is available in the Appendix at the end of this book, where you can get some idea of the total comparative costs of post-secondary education in a number of countries.

A) Tuition fees

There is a tremendous variation in the cost of attending a post-secondary institution, and there are many factors which affect what you will actually pay. The two biggest determining factors are: (1) the policy of the country you are going to study in concerning who is actually responsible for paying what it will cost the institution to provide you with an education and (2) the nature of the institution itself—whether it is publicly supported by money raised from the taxpayers, or whether it is funded privately so that all its costs are paid for by its own revenues.

In the most expensive scenarios, usually those of private universities in the United States, the tuition fees alone can reach US$20,000 a year or even higher, whereas in some countries where the university system is totally supported by the government (Germany, for example), there is no charge at all to the student for attending. What you will actually have to pay for studying overseas will most likely fall somewhere between these two ends, but there is no accurate method with which to calculate the exact amount.

☛ *The only way to find out specific costs is to write in and ask the university or institution you want to attend, and make sure when you do that you are given the fee schedule for an overseas student, as many universities have two fee scales-one for nationals of the country, who are partly supported by revenue from taxes raised in that country, and another for foreign students for whom the universities receive no subsidy.*

B) Examination fees

Not all universities charge these as some absorb them into the overall tuition fee structure, or into the student activity fees. To make sure, you should ask, at the same time you enquire about tuition fees, whether or not there are any additional fees of an academic nature, such as examination fees. If you do not make it a point to check beforehand, you may be in for a nasty shock at the end of your first academic year, when your money supply is usually at its lowest!

C) Student activity fees

A number of post-secondary institutions charge an additional fee, at the time that you pay your academic fees, for what is often known as "student interests". This covers a wide range of activities and services to which you will have automatic access during your time as a student, but which are not specifically academic in nature. These can include publications, such as the newspaper and/or yearbook, services such as counselling, international student advising, transportation (if there is a free campus bus service), the use of facilities such as the sports complex or the student centre, as well as extracurricular activities such as the various clubs and societies on the campus that often derive much of their operating budget from these student fees. The amount that you pay varies with the institution but is often about 10%-20% of the tuition fees. You will not usually have an option on whether to pay or not because the student fees are collected at the same time that you pay your tuition fees and then reallocated directly by the university to the areas in which the money is to be spent.

D) Books and supplies

Once again, the amount you will have to pay will vary both with the country you are studying in (depending on the overall cost of books there) and what course of study you are following. Generally, students in engineering and medicine will pay more than others, because their books are bigger and more specialised, and there are often additional fees for laboratory use. Most students, however, can expect to see no change from the equivalent of US$1,000 a year, at least for their required books. Students in courses where supplies are needed for study purposes in addition to books (in art and architecture, for instance) can expect to pay even more as there will be additional expenses in such courses. It is sometimes possible to save a little money on books by buying them second-hand when you arrive on the campus, but this cannot be counted on as second-hand copies are not always available. Even if they are, you will have to check if those used in previous years are still being used in the year of your study.

E) Room and board
What level of comfort are you looking for and how much do you eat? The answers to these questions will largely determine how much room and board will cost you, as will your choice of whether you live and eat in a university residence or in a place of your own away from campus. It is hard to quote a general cost, but it will probably not be less than US$5,000 a year at any North American campus, regardless of what you choose to do.

Residence accommodation is usually available at most post-secondary places of study, but often only in double rooms. Whatever single rooms there are often tend to be very small, and the whole atmosphere is quite noisy. They can often be more expensive, too, than finding a room outside the campus to live in by yourself or sharing an apartment with other students—but once again, that depends on the lifestyle you want.

Nearly all universities have housing departments to help you understand what your options are in terms of room and board, and many of these will also help you find people to share accommodation with, if you request it of them.

F) Health Insurance
It is imperative that you have some form of health insurance to cover you while you are away studying. Anybody can get sick or have an accident and the cost of medical care can be extremely high in some countries if you have to pay for it yourself. Some post-secondary institutions have their own plans that will provide you with medical coverage—for an additional cost, of

course—but many do not and it is up to you to arrange your own health coverage, either through private insurance in your own country before you leave, or through insurers in the country to which you are going. You may even be asked for proof of your medical insurance before you are given a student visa to the country in which you propose to study, as no country wants to admit someone who can potentially become a large drain on its medical system.

For minor ailments, many universities maintain a small clinic on the campus and the medical service that it provides is usually free as it is subsidised by the student activity funds. For major illnesses, however, health insurance coverage is a must!

G) Travel

There are several types of travel that you may want to undertake while you are away studying. The most obvious is actually getting to the place where you are going to study and returning home from there when you are finished—plus any holidays you plan to take at home in between. But there is also local travel—getting around to see the country in which you are living and visiting friends there, as well as simply getting to your classes and back if you live off the campus. Once again, what all this will cost you will depend on how much and how often you actually move around but, as it can be a sizeable sum, an amount for travel should certainly be built into your estimate of the overall cost of attending a post-secondary institution overseas.

H) Personal allowance

This is the most difficult cost of all to estimate as it depends on how you plan to live. This amount also includes a whole variety of little things for which you might have to pay on a regular basis—laundry, going to the cinema, sending letters home, buying presents, attending functions and so on. Few students can manage to live on less than US$2,000 a year in North America, although it is not impossible. However, when you are calculating this amount, it is better to err on the generous side as there is nothing worse than running out of spending money halfway through the year and having to survive with no money at all for the other half. How you budget your personal money is half the trick, but the other half is making sure that the amount you have can support the kind of lifestyle you plan to lead.

SCHOLARSHIPS AND AWARDS

There are several categories of scholarships and awards that are commonly available at post-secondary institutions. Not every institution will have all of the following, but the vast majority will have some of them. When you are making initial enquiries of the universities you are interested in, you should ask them to send you information on all the awards programmes they offer and the method by which you can apply for them. In the Appendix at the end of this book, there is also an extensive list of publications which deal specifically with scholarships, grants, awards and other kinds of financial aid.

A) Automatic entry scholarships

These scholarships are awarded by institutions automatically once they have decided upon the people they are going to admit in a particular year. Many places have a number of financial awards—either in cash or in the form of fee reductions—that they offer to new students with the highest academic standing. These cannot be applied for as they are based solely on academic criteria. You can find out how many of these scholarships are available at a particular institution by asking the admissions office, but you will not know whether or not you have been awarded one until your admission has been confirmed and, of course, any such offer you receive will only be valid at that particular institution. Should you decide not to go there, you will have to forfeit your scholarship offer.

B) Specific university scholarships

The automatic entry awards may not be the only awards that a particular university hands out. There are usually a number of others for which there are specific criteria—the place you live, the profession of your parents, your personal background, an extracurricular strength and so forth, but you will have to apply for these as the university will not have enough information on you initially to know whether you are eligible or not.

Once again, it is important that you ask the institutions for a list of this kind of scholarship in advance, so that you know what possibilities exist there for you. Be warned, however, that some of these scholarships have restrictions on them and may not be available to students who are not nationals of the host country.

C) Athletic scholarships

This is probably one of the best-known kinds of scholarship—at least in the United States, where a number of them exist. There are two things to be aware of concerning athletic scholarships: (1) you have to be extremely good in your chosen sport (often near-professional in standard) and have a strong recommendation from your current coach and (2) they are not offered by all universities and, in some countries, not at all.

If you are a very good sports person and you think that you might qualify for an athletic scholarship in your sport somewhere, you should start making enquiries very early about places that have strong teams in that field and contact the coach at that institution—or have your own coach do it—before you begin the application process. There are a number of books available which list universities in the United States that offer these scholarships (*The College Handbook from the College Board*, for instance) and they are worth getting hold of and consulting in advance.

D) Need-based bursaries

These are not scholarships in the strict sense of the word as they are not awarded on the basis of academic competition, but rather on the basis of the ability to pay. As mentioned earlier, some universities take this into consideration during the application process and some do not but, at both kinds of institutions, there are sometimes bursaries which can be offered to students who have strong academic backgrounds but whose ability to go and study there may depend on getting some kind of financial help. These bursaries are usually open for application and will often require an examination by the institution of your financial situation (and, if appropriate, that of your parents) before they are awarded.

E) Loan programmes—national, local and institution-based

Most countries have some kind of national loan plan for students who are qualified to go on to post-secondary institutions but who need the money to be able to do so. In most cases, this loan is interest-free with the money having to be repaid after graduation, but there are a number of variants of this basic plan. The main problem with national loans is that they sometimes cannot be accessed if you are going to study out of your home country, while the country you are going to does not offer them to students who come from overseas! In situations like this, there is little you can do, but you can check if there are local or institution-based loan programmes for which you can qualify.

Local loan programmes may be offered by the region or municipality in which you live or by the area in which you will be living, but it will be up to you to check on this. Post-secondary institutions sometimes have loan programmes for their own students which are not restricted to nationals of that country but again, you will have to check with them on this, both for availability and for the maximum amount you can receive if you qualify under any such plan. You should be aware that all public loan programmes usually have means tests associated with them— that is, some way of establishing that you really do need the money—and that if your income or that of your parents is considered too high, you may not qualify for any.

OTHER SOURCES OF MONEY
A) Through self-funded scholarships
Some countries have non-profit plans in which parents can invest early in their child's life (often before the age of six) and pay an annual sum from then until the time at which the child is eligible to attend a post-secondary institution (or sometimes, when the child reaches the age of 18). At this point the principal sum invested is returned—but with no interest. The interest which would have been paid on this money over the years is deposited into a central fund from which the scholarships are paid to those students who actually attend qualified post-secondary institutions.

Technically, these are not scholarships at all, as they have no connection with the academic ability of the student, but merely take into account the fact that they qualify to attend, and then remain at, an eligible post-secondary institution. The catch with these plans is, of course, that they are a gamble that has to be taken early in a child's life because, if that child does not eventually attend a post-secondary educational institution, only the principal sum is returned and the interest on that money has been lost for all of the 12 years or so that it has been invested. However, plans such as these are quite popular and do help those who have them—but if you are already 18 and looking for financial support for some place, you are too late for this one!

B) Through the armed forces
Some countries will subsidise—or even fully finance—the post-secondary education of students who are willing to make a predetermined commitment to serve in the armed forces of that country after graduation. The catch here is that such programmes are highly sought after and competitive and they are often not

available to students who are planning to study out of the country. But it is worth checking on if a military career is on the cards, as the amounts involved can often be substantial.

C) Through financial institutions

Increasingly, private financial institutions such as banks or trust companies are offering loan programmes for students. These are, of course, not interest-free in the way that public loans often are, but they are available at reasonably good rates and can be attractive to students who do not qualify financially for public loan programmes, but still need some help to pay all the costs associated with studying in a university.

D) Through sponsorship

This is not an easy category in which to find money, but there are places and people who are willing to sponsor university study. Large companies sometimes have sponsorship plans for the children of their employees, as do foundations and agencies that work with specific kinds of people, as well as organisations to which someone in your family may belong.

☞   *There is no easy way of locating a possible sponsor—unless you are already aware of one—but check the various companies and organisations to which you or your parents belong and see whether there are any plans which can help you to meet your financial needs.*

E) Through relatives and friends

It is amazing how often your old Auntie Flo will be willing to help out with university costs if she is asked—and often equally as amazing to realise the kind of money she has available with which to do this! Older people are often quite willing, upon polite request, to help the younger members of the family get started, if they are able to do so.

WORKING WHILE YOU STUDY
A) Summer work (home country)

It is almost a tradition in North America that post-secondary students will find jobs and work during the long summer break. Since most places finish the academic year by the end of April, this can mean that four months or longer is available for full-time work, during which quite a substantial amount of money can be earned. The first step, of course, is finding a job to work at and, in the current economic climate, this can sometimes be quite difficult. However, there are summer jobs out there—some of them quite well paying—if you apply early enough and are not too fussy about the kind of work you are willing to accept.

☞   *Overseas students should be a little cautious here, as employment regulations in the country in which they are studying may restrict or even prevent employment. This should be thoroughly investigated before starting on any form of employment as contravention of such a regulation—even as a result of ignorance—may result in the student visa being revoked! Of course, there is nothing to stop a student from returning home to his or her own country and working there for the long summer break—if jobs are available.*

B) On-campus work (university-based)

Many universities offer work/study opportunities where a student will be offered a part-time job on the campus where he or she is studying (in the library or the computer centre, for instance) up to a certain number of hours a week, for which the student will be paid. In certain cases, this kind of employment does not require a special permit—or, if it does, the university will get it for you—but in others it does, and this should be checked upon for the reason given above. If working on campus is both permissible and available, this is often a very good way to subsidise the cost of your studies as it does not intrude too much into the time available for study, and it provides you with another perspective of the institution in which you are studying.

C) Off-campus work (non-university based)

This is often available to students in the general area surrounding the university and includes work which can range from pumping gas and working in a restaurant to tutoring and part-time teaching. The majority of such jobs, however, require either nationality of the country concerned or a permit to work there, and this should be checked out very carefully before taking on any job outside the campus. Running foul of the authorities can have very drastic consequences that will affect your ability to complete your studies in that country!

D) Self-employment (typing, tutoring and so on)

This is an often neglected way of raising some money while studying. There are always services which you can offer to your fellow students if you have the skills to do so—such as typing essays, tutoring in a specific subject or coaching in a sport—and for which the individual student you help will be willing to pay you. Since these are private arrangements and confined to the campus, they do not usually require an employment permit but, if you are concerned about not running foul of regulations, you can always check with the university authorities before you begin to offer any such services.

Chapter Five

READY, SET, GO!

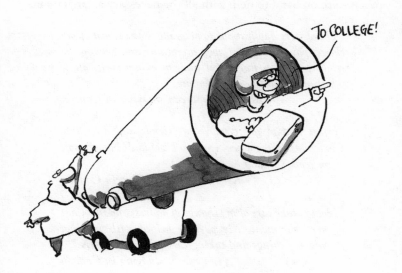

Now that you have chosen your university and course of study, arranged for financing, and obtained your student visa, you are ready to go. Having decided upon your course of study, make sure you are adequately prepared for and informed about it. It is helpful to speak with people who have been to the college or university you will be attending. Also spend your time learning about the culture, values and customs of that country.

ORGANISING YOUR PERSONAL AFFAIRS
Most students planning to go overseas to study at the under-graduate level will have very few personal affairs to be taken care of as they will be going almost immediately after finishing school.

If you are such a student, organising your personal affairs may mean nothing more than tidying up your room, sorting through your books and personal effects, and stashing away those things that you do not need to take along with you. In many cases, parents are on hand to help with all the necessary arrangements.

> *"There were applications to be made to the school of my choice, payment of fees upon acceptance and getting the student visa, airline ticket and an exit permit, all of which my Mum handled for me."*
> —*DR, a Singaporean studying in Canada*

> *"I just had to say goodbye to friends and distribute Christmas presents very early so I wouldn't have to post them from Canada."*
> —*KW, a Briton studying in Canada*

> *"I had to take care of my change of address and move out of my apartment. My parents helped with moving, storing my things and taking care of bank matters."*
> —*AJ, a Swede studying in Canada*

If you are working, you will have to hand in your resignation, giving your employer adequate notice. Then you will have to complete your assignments in readiness for your departure. In some workplaces, it is possible to apply for extended leave without pay, especially if your course of study will not take longer than a year to complete.

☞ *If you do have to resign, remember to get good references from your employer to take along with you. These will come in handy should you decide to apply for summer or part-time jobs while studying.*

Exchange students will have to ensure that their course of

study in the foreign university is recognised by their home university.

> *"The most important task I had before leaving was determining which classes at Waseda University would be recognised at Stanford with regard to being able to use those credits. I did not want to have to spend an extra year at Stanford because I took a year to study abroad. I obtained a list of courses available to me at Waseda, tentatively picked out the ones I was interested in, and went around to all the appropriate professors at Stanford to get their approval. Upon my return to Stanford, I was actually able to transfer almost all of the credits for the classes I took at Waseda, and ended up graduating two months early."*
> —*YP, an American who studied in Japan*

Try to learn a little more about the country you will be living in for some time. Go to your town library, the consulate or embassy's resource centre and wherever you are able to obtain relevant information. Many people are fairly well-travelled these days, so you should seek information from relatives and friends who have either been to the country you are heading for, or a country that has a similar climate and culture. You can also get tips from people who have studied abroad. Some universities have an alumni association of former students in your country who are willing to provide support and information about their own experiences. Culture shock can be substantially reduced if you have some idea of what you will be facing.

WHAT STAYS, WHAT GOES?
Most airlines allow only two luggage bags with a weight limitation of 32 kg each on board the plane. Dilemma: how do you fit your whole life up till now into it? The answer is: you do not. All

you need are the basics to start you off in your student life, although this will vary from person to person. If you are a firm believer in travelling light, one maxim you can follow is: you can always buy it there! And if you cannot, you can probably live without it.

It is comforting to have some familiar, well-loved items surrounding you when you are in a strange environment. The little space that huggable soft toy (don't we all have one?) occupies in one luggage bag is worth every cubic centimeter when homesickness strikes. But do not bring the whole soft toy department along with you. Whatever else you choose to fill the rest of your luggage, remember that if you forget something, you can either buy it or send for it later.

When you go shopping for clothes, try to avoid the common mistake of overbuying. This is especially true for those who will be going from a tropical to a temperate climate. It is best if you can time it so that you arrive when the weather is still warm.

This gives you some time to acclimatise and, as the weather cools, you will be able to buy the warmer clothes that you need. Moreover, stores selling winter clothing are scarce in a tropical country, and what they do sell may be so out of fashion in your host country that wearing these home-bought clothes may only set you further apart from those around you.

If you are fortunate, you may have friends or relatives who have been overseas. Seek their advice on what to expect. They may even be willing to lend you some of their warm clothing. This is much better than buying as you cannot be sure that what you buy is the correct thing to have but, again, here is a warning: while it is important to be properly protected against the cold, do not bring too much. That seasoned traveller's rule—to pack lightly, then go through the bags and throw out half of what was in it—applies here too.

> *"We expected the winter to be very cold, so we brought a lot of bulky clothes to wear inside the house. But the insulation in the house was far more advanced than we had expected, so we did not need to wear so much."*
> *—YH, a Japanese who lived in Toronto, Canada*

The problem of what clothes to bring is probably greater for a person travelling from a warm climate to a cold one. But a student from Canada going to Thailand, for instance, should also try to find out not only what is comfortable, but also what is acceptable wear there.

As for food, it is best if you make up your mind to eat "locally" but for this first trip, do put in a few well-loved and favourite snacks to help comfort you as you adjust to your new life. Be sure, however, that you check with the airline or customs authorities of the country about what food items you can bring in and what are prohibited. Highly agricultural countries like Australia, New Zealand and Canada are extremely cautious about the possibility of travellers bringing unwelcome "bugs" into their country.

If you do not have any photographs of your family and close friends, now is the time to get them and place them into small picture frames that you can set up in your room or on your desk. Such little touches help to give a more familiar feeling to a strange environment.

Be prepared to share information about your country and what life is like "back home". This is especially important if you are an exchange student. Take along the words to some national songs or songs with a local flavour, a national costume or its equivalent to wear, and photographs and slides of your country and people. Do not forget, too, to take with you a few souvenirs from your country—like stickers, badges or pins with a national emblem. These do not take up much space and are relatively inexpensive. They will come in handy when you have to attend gatherings with an international or multi-cultural flavour.

> "Every year, my school had an International Day dur-
> ing which we were encouraged to dress in our national
> or cultural costumes. I always wore my Singapore Girl
> uniform on those days."—GC, a Singapore student in a
> Canadian high school

Music is an important part of most people's lives. You will probably want to take a portable radio or stereo set along. If electrical and electronic goods are relatively cheap in your own country, you can take such items along with you rather than buy. Do be careful to check, though, that the goods can be used in your host country. Adaptors may be required. For instance, the voltage of most electrical appliances is 110/120 volts in Canada, and this is compatible with that in the United States. However, Australia and England use 220/240 volts, and this is also the case in Singapore and Malaysia.

Do you require special medication, or suffer from allergies? Make a note of any special medical requirements you might have, or even get a note from your family doctor and take along a small supply of any special medicines you have to take in order to tide you over the initial settling-in period. Make a record of your prescription spectacles, if you wear them. If you are an active person and plan to take part in sports, getting an extra pair of spectacles will be a good move.

The following are some things that were forgotten or could not be taken along, and were sadly missed by their owners:

> *"My favourite jacket and my boyfriend."*

> *"What I couldn't bring was my stereo—too big—and I really missed it."*

> *"Stereo system, photo albums."*

> *"Should have brought more clothes. There is little time for shopping."*

> *"My friends' addresses. I forgot to ask for them."*

> *"A hockey net to practise with."*

A CHECKLIST

Depending on how long you will be away, the number of things you have to pack will differ quite radically. An undergraduate planning at least three to four years of study for a first degree will have much more than two luggage bags can carry. Things taken along on the initial trip will probably be supplemented by parcels from home, or brought in by visiting relatives and friends. On the other hand, an exchange student, someone who is pursuing a special course like a foreign language, or a graduate student, can pack less to take along.

"I took only two suitcases. I had clothes for all seasons, one biochemistry book, a Walkman and some tapes. I didn't forget anything."—ZQ, a Canadian graduate student who spent a year in the United Kingdom

☞ **Whatever your situation, it helps to make yourself a checklist like this, adding items to it whenever you think of something you should not forget to take with you:**

Clothes for all seasons (according to your needs)
Toiletries
Snacks
Favourite soft toy
Walkman
Souvenirs
Family photos
Information on your home country
National or ethnic dress
Special medication
Extra prescription lenses
... and so on.

SAYING GOODBYE

This is always a bittersweet affair. During this time, you are the most important person around—friends and relatives hold going-away parties for you, you get lots of presents and enjoy being the centre of attention. Do not forget to have an address book in which to note the addresses of friends. You may not think yourself much of a letter writer but, being far away from home will often change your perspective on the matter.

These days, though, finances permitting, keeping in touch with people on opposite ends of the globe is just a phone call or a fascimile away. So when you are jotting down those addresses, do not forget to get telephone and fax numbers as well!

When the time to leave comes, some people like to have large crowds with them at the airport while others prefer to slip away quietly. Whatever your preference, make it known to your family and friends.

> *"It took me about a week to say a decent goodbye to my closest friends. I requested that they should not go to the airport for fear of a soppy family scene. Besides, I hate goodbyes. The immediate family came to the airport and, thankfully, it wasn't a tearful parting."*
>
> —DR, *a Singaporean in Canada*

Practically speaking, having too many people see you off at the airport can cause quite a confusion. You would have said most of your goodbyes at farewell parties. Save the airport scene for family and a few close friends.

> *"I went out with friends and family a lot before I left. I had dinner out every night for about two to four weeks before my departure. A lot of family members and friends sent me off at the airport."*
>
> —CLT, *a Singaporean in Canada*

ARRIVING IN YOUR HOST COUNTRY

Some institutions will arrange for a representative to meet you at the airport, train station or other point of entry. If not, you may have to manage on your own right from the beginning. It may mean taking a train, taxi or bus to your place of accommodation. If you have a home stay, your host family may be at the airport to greet you.

> *"I had arranged for my air ticket reservation and my journey from Narita Airport by train to the university.*

> *I made my own way to the guest dormitory before being*
> *assigned to a host family. While in Japan, I travelled*
> *mostly on trains and learned by getting lost and asking*
> *a lot of questions."*
> —*DP, an American who studied in Japan*

Sometimes, the international students' organisation in the country will arrange to meet arriving students and ease them into their new life.

> *"Volunteers from the international students' group met*
> *me and other new students at the airport. We shared a*
> *hotel room that first night."*—*AJ, Swede in Canada*

If you are fortunate, your parents may accompany you on this important trip and see that you are properly settled in and that your needs are taken care of during this period.

> *"We rented a car in San Francisco and my father drove*
> *us to Stockton, where I would be studying."*
> —*LSY, a Singaporean in the United States*

Others may have friends or relatives living in the host country. This eases the transition period as there will often be someone familiar to meet you at the airport, and you will have a home to go to for a few days or weeks before school begins.

> *"My grandparents took me to the airport in Vancouver.*
> *I flew from Vancouver to Heathrow and, in London,*
> *my aunt picked me up."*
> —*ZQ, Canadian who studied in England*

As far as possible, try to be in your host country a little earlier before school begins. This will give you some time to adjust to the new environment and climate before you have to deal with the added elements of adjusting to a new school or university, teachers and fellow students. In North America, where the school and university year begins in September, scheduling your trip in late August gives you an opportunity to acclimatise before the cooler weather and winter sets in.

ORIENTATION

Now, you finally find yourself settling into a new culture and climate. You have to deal with the anxieties that the experience of being in a new learning environment creates. When you received your acceptance into the institution of learning, you probably also received a lot of information about orientation programmes that have been organised for newcomers.

Ideally, orientation should begin before you even leave home. Orientation programmes for departing students may be conducted by the representatives of the host country (such as consulate officials), your own government (particularly if you are a sponsored student) or by the private institutions.

The institution you are joining should give you information about how much money you will require, health and accident insurance, immigration regulations, registration procedures and transportation information.

☞ *Make sure you attend the orientation courses or tours that have been organised.*

Some universities, recognising the importance of such orientation activities, make it compulsory. Tours will familiarise you with the campus so that you know where the various faculties, lecture halls and classrooms are and the amenities available. Your orientation should include learning how to use campus facilities effectively, such as the library and the laboratory, where you will be spending much of your time.

This is also the time when you meet a lot of other new students and get to know some of the people who will be taking the same courses as you and, if you are living in a residence on campus, you will get to meet the people with whom you will share living space.

Besides giving you specific information to help you adjust to the campus and introduce you to support services for foreign students—such as the international student adviser or counsellor—a good orientation programme will include information to increase your knowledge and understanding of the system of education you are now entering, as well as the culture, values and customs of the people who will be your hosts.

Students' unions often have committees whose task is to help new arrivals like you settle into your new environment with as little pain as possible. On some campuses, a "buddy system", which pairs an experienced student with one who has just arrived, helps the new student to adapt more quickly. It will also give the new student an established circle of contacts that will help him or her to feel less isolated.

Chapter Six

FITTING INTO THE CULTURE

YOU'LL FIT IN PERFECTLY SON...
AAGH! OXFORD'S NOT IN SCOTLAND

There are many adjustment problems that foreign students have to cope with. You will definitely have to get used to making many decisions on your own, without the benefit of support from family and friends. In addition, you may have problems with the language that may make your studies more difficult. Cultural differences also come into play and you will have to deal with the very obvious feeling of being different, a stranger in a foreign land. You will have to adapt to all these new situations.

Your personality will be an important factor in how well you adapt and handle such problems. Naturally, if you are flexible, friendly and mix easily with people, you will be able to adapt better.

MAKING FRIENDS

One of the basic needs of a person is to have the love and security provided by family and friends. However, you are now far removed from such warmth and comfort, and in an unfamiliar environment.

☛ *It is important to develop some friendships so that your time abroad is a happy one in which you feel you belong and are part of a group. If you are studying in a large university, there can be a feeling of being lost and alienated.*

The problem of making friends is a particularly difficult one for a much younger student whose family has had to relocate and who has to adjust to studying overseas at the primary or secondary school level. Teens and pre-teens can be less tolerant of differences. Yet this is the age when having a friend and being accepted is extremely important. If you are the only one in the class who is different, this can be a trying situation.

> *"I spoke with an accent and the school kids found it strange. They also found it strange that a Chinese could speak English so well. They would tease me because I was different, and I think they also felt uneasy around me."—GC, a Chinese in a Canadian elementary school*

If, however, it is by choice that you are alone, or if you have decided that your time abroad has to be spent concentrating on study and work, you can be quite happy too because you are alone by choice. But, without a doubt, studying overseas is a more satisfying experience if you take this opportunity to develop friendships with people from other countries and learn more about their cultures. For some students, especially those who have gone abroad specifically with the intention of immersing themselves in the culture of the country, this is a part of their goal.

"I made friends largely through the International House on campus, my roommates and people I met in classes. My friends are largely local students because those were the people I travelled all this way to meet. But I also have overseas students as friends."
—*KW, a Briton studying in Canada*

Making friends can be extremely difficult. When you make the acquaintance of someone, there is no substitute for a genuine and sympathetic interest in that person, and in wanting to know him or her better. Try to participate in conversations and keep the talk away from yourself. Make it a point to know what people are interested in and bring these subjects into the conversation. If you have a wide range of interests and read widely, you will be an interesting person to know. Do remember that you should never gossip, criticise or make disparaging remarks about others.

Here is advice from students who have been through it all:

"Establish bonds with other students right away. Spend time with them and invite them over in the first week."—*ZQ, a Canadian in England*

"Don't isolate yourself or keep to yourself or your group. When in public, don't talk in a foreign language. Show others that you respect their culture by speaking in their language instead of your own. Move around, show interest in other cultures."
—*DP, a Singaporean in Australia*

"Be outgoing, sociable. The last thing you can be is shy."—*YH, a Japanese in Canada*

"Go to orientations and don't be shy! People don't always make the first move."
—*SB, a Indonesian in Canada*

Opportunities to socialise are plentiful, especially if you live in residence or belong to a club or sorority. Residences, faculties, departments, societies, clubs and houses all organise many social events, activities and games—so many, in fact, that you may get caught up in the whirl of activities to the extent of neglecting your studies. You will soon find out which societies are the ones to join, and which pub or lounge you should go to in order to be part of the "in" group. Do not be shy.

Remember, however, that the concept of friendship differs from one culture to another. In some cultures, it is a very deep relationship that is experienced with very few people because it is based on love and respect and demands unlimited obligations. In another culture, friendship is understood to mean just doing things with people whose company one enjoys. For example, Americans are described by foreign students as very friendly and approachable, but difficult to really get to know. Americans use expressions such as "Come on over some time", "I'll call you", and "Let's get together some time", as pleasantries and may not necessarily follow through with them. But the foreign student from another culture where friendship is more permanent and lasting takes these invitations to be signs of sincere interest and are disappointed when this is not the case.

To be sure, foreign students generally find it easier to form warm, dependent and more satisfying friendships with others from their own country, or with other international students. This is so especially if there are language difficulties. Foreign students do participate with locals, they may share project work, socialise or even room together, but these relationships rarely go beyond friendly but casual encounters.

Often, some colleges or universities are popular with students from a particular country, and it is therefore easy to find many other students who come from your own country so that you could spend three or four years in a foreign country and yet not make any "foreign" friends. Be a little careful about this, however, as confining yourself to friendships with people who have backgrounds similar to yours is not always the most sensible approach. In some ways, it negates the whole reason for your choosing to study overseas in the first place!

> *"I associated with fellow Asian students during my first year. This was labelled as the "Chinatown" by others and it was not a pleasant thing. However, I distanced myself from "Chinatown" during my second year and mixed mostly with the locals. That was a decision I did not regret."* —RF, a Singaporean in Canada

LANGUAGE DIFFERENCES AND DIFFICULTIES

Difficulties with the language is one of the most common concerns that foreign students have. It is better to choose a course of study in a country where you can speak the language because it will mean one less problem for you. Sometimes, however, this is not possible—when the move is the result of your family being transferred to another country, for example—and if you have no knowledge of the language, you will probably have to take special language classes to help you cope with this difficulty.

> *"I dove right in, staring with the word "goal" in German, and I was in an immersion programme. My advice is if it is a foreign tongue for you, dedicate half of a year to prepare for it."*
> —RDS, Canadian who studied in Germany

Besides taking extra lessons in school, additional tutoring or attending summer school will help you to catch up with the language. Total immersion in the language and culture of the country will hasten your ability to speak the language. In the meantime, you will be surprised at how much you can communicate through sign language.

85

"I took language classes and tried my best, with the help
of sign language and lots of patience."
—*DP, an American who studied in Japan*

In some countries, the language of the local community is not the same as the language of instruction in the university. For instance, if you study in McGill University in Montreal, Canada, you will be learning in English but, at the same time, you should be able to communicate in French, which is the dominant language of the community at large. Similarly, you may study in English or even Mandarin in a Hong Kong university but, to function outside the campus, it is important to know Cantonese.

Some students of a second language or a culture deliberately seek immersion because they wish to experience the language or culture at source. Learning the language in a class environment is totally different from experiencing it in its natural setting.

Most of the time though, you will want to study in a country where you can speak the language. Even so, there are differences in the meanings and uses of words that can be quite unexpected. For instance, in North America, if you have a little cut on a finger and go into a pharmacy asking for "plaster", you will not be understood because the item you require is known as "band aid".

In a restaurant, you would not ask for a "soft drink" when it is really "pop" that you want and when your meal is over, do not ask for the "bill" because it is really a "check". You give "candy" to a child, not "sweets". Shopping at the stationers can also be confusing until you learn to recognise that the "folder" is a "file" here, while a "file" is a "binder".

Sometimes, the wrong choice of words can lead to embarrassing situations. One seemingly innocuous word to avoid in the United States and Canada is "rubber". If you wish to erase a mistake on the written page, ask for an "eraser" and not a "rubber", which is a slang word for "condom". However, this is a mistake that you will probably make only once!

Most of the time, these are not serious obstacles to understanding and after getting accustomed to the difference in accents, you will very quickly learn the words and expressions that are peculiar to the country you are in.

Some foreign students have more serious difficulties with the language. Before admission into their educational institutions, some countries in which English is the operative language conduct tests to ensure that foreign students are able to cope with the language. (A more detailed discussion on this can be found in Chapter Two.) However, these tests are designed to ascertain only if the foreign student meets the minimum institutional requirements and are no guarantee that the student will not have any difficulty with the language of study. Even those who have been educated in an English-language school find reading and writing in English quite different at university level. Language difficulties will affect a student's ability to do reading assignments and answer essay questions. Understanding lectures, discussions and instructions may also be a problem, particularly if the lecturer speaks rapidly and in an unfamiliar accent. Language problems also inhibit the student from expressing an opinion in class, and limits contact with professors and other students.

THE CLASSROOM SITUATION

Formal or informal? While this depends on which university you go to and in which country, dress in most universities tends to be casual—jeans, T-shirts, sweat shirts and even shorts, weather permitting!

Classroom atmosphere and teacher-student relationships also tend to be more informal in North America. If you are used to a formal atmosphere in school—where uniforms are the norm; cosmetics are not allowed; rules exist regarding length and style of hair and colour of shoes; teachers are addressed as Miss, Mrs or Mr So-and-So and never as Linda, Frank or Ralph; and students do not talk in class, contradict the teacher, argue or debate very much, then you may be in for a shock. In western societies, students are used to a more egalitarian society. Most have never worn a school uniform in their 10 years or more of primary and secondary education. You will find that they do not stand in awe of their teachers and being on a first-name basis with the teacher is not unusual.

You will probably have to adjust to a different method of teaching. Instead of a classroom type of situation, you will attend lectures together with more than a hundred other students. At the other end of the scale, you will also have to take part in tutorials and seminars involving small groups of people and you will be expected to debate and discuss along with the rest.

> *"No attendance was taken in class. I had to learn self-discipline and not to feel intimidated when I wanted to raise a question in a large lecture hall. My advice is to try not to skip classes too much."—CCY, a Singaporean who studied in the United States*

> *"There was more application studying than just plain memorising. Classes were informal and the professors very easy-going."—SS, a Singaporean in Canada*

If, in your culture, you are accustomed to not questioning your elders or superiors or are unused to the idea of speaking up and expressing your opinion, to be thrown into a learning environment where students are outspoken and challenge their teachers is a cultural shock for you. In order not to "lose face" you may answer "yes" or pretend to understand.

Methods of study may also be different. You will have to learn to do your own research and study. You will have to read more than the prescribed textbooks and consult journals and other reference materials. There may be less emphasis on memorising material, and more on developing the ability of synthesising information for the purpose of formulating your own ideas.

The relationship between student and staff may also take some getting used to. Professors may remain after class and hold informal, serious discussions with their students or even occasionally invite students to their homes. This would be unusual for students who have never experienced having any contact with teaching staff outside of the classroom. On the other hand, a foreign student who is used to such familiarity would find any formality in the classroom situation and student-faculty relationship somewhat strange.

"I found the learning environment at my university quite different from what I had been used to. There was a course outline given for each course, and final examinations were worth only a certain percentage. Professors were addressed by their first names. I had to keep my eyes and ears open."—CLT, a Singaporean in Canada

"One of my law classes is a workshop, which is much less formal than at home. No tutorials accompany lectures here, which is a shame, because I found these helpful at home. Despite warnings to the contrary, I found that being an undergrad in a grad department was not a problem."—KW, a Briton in Canada

"I was not used to doing courses in parallel with one another. I was used to doing one after the other. It was stressful and I was not prepared for the amount of work. The classes were much bigger than what I was used to and slightly more formal."—AJ, a Swede in Canada

DEALING WITH HOMESICKNESS

Some students who go overseas to study do so because their whole family has gone abroad. This may be due to a job transfer or the family emigrating. There will be fewer problems with adjusting to a new environment but homesickness is not just about missing family and friends.

It is also to do with having to adjust to a totally different environment—for instance, if your studies abroad have meant a move from a big city to a small town, or vice versa. If you are used to the amenities and entertainment available in a big urban centre and then have to adjust to living in a small community, being deprived of the places you like to visit—such as cinemas, theatres and shops—can add to a feeling of loneliness and alienation. Just being in a quiet environment where the pace of life seems much slower needs a lot of getting used to.

One student found the "sounds of silence" so overwhelming at times that he resorted to tape-recording the sounds of city living on his next visit home so that he could play it back whenever the silence became too much to bear!

But as centres of study tend to be in the bigger communities, there will be more students who will find that a large part of homesickness has to do with adjusting to the noise, a faster pace of living and, perhaps, missing the wide open spaces of home.

If you are moving into a culture that is totally different from your own, you may find that being constantly surrounded by people who look and speak so differently from you can be quite a shock to your system. You will very quickly pick out others who, like you, may be the odd ones in the crowd and gravitate towards them for companionship.

> *"I was very excited to be abroad but, at the same time,
> it was also the first time I was so far away from home.
> No doubt, I felt homesick that year in Japan but I knew
> I was only going to be there for a short period of nine*

months, so I just decided to make the most of it. Making friends with other American students in the programme greatly helped ease the loneliness of being in a foreign country, so I think it's important to make those connections."—YP, an American student in Japan

Studying overseas, however, does not necessarily mean that it has to be done in an environment that is totally foreign. It can be a country that is culturally similar in some ways to yours—for example, if you are an American going to study in Canada or a Canadian going to study in England. You may be going to a country that you have visited before, as a tourist perhaps, or you may have relatives living there. You will not be entirely free from being homesick, but will experience it to a lesser degree.

If, however, you are not so fortunate as to have your family with you while studying overseas and you expect to be thrown into a completely alien culture and environment, you will have to brace yourself to deal with the feelings of loneliness and alienation that will surface from time to time. There are different ways of dealing with this but they all boil down to one thing—keeping active and involved.

This can be done by keeping busy with work; making friends from your own country, your host country and other international students; being involved in extracurricular activities and, as far as possible, doing the things you like, such as listening to music.

The knowledge that there will be an end to this, that it is but a temporary phase in your life, helps to sustain you. If finances permit, frequent phone calls home are extremely helpful—but limit the number of calls you make when you first arrive to give yourself a fair chance to settle into the new environment without remaining overly dependent on your own!

"I called home a lot. My monthly phone bills came to

> C$200 or more, excluding the times when my family
> called me!"—CLT, a Singaporean in Canada

> "I felt better when I kept busy with work, making
> friends, exercising and listening to music."
> —ZQ, a Canadian in England

> "I felt very homesick. I visited with friends, who were
> mainly Singaporeans, and kept busy generally."—LSY,
> a Singaporean who studied in the United States

COPING WITH THE CLIMATE

Something has already been said in the previous chapter about
preparing yourself for a different kind of climate. It is easier to
adjust to a climate that is warmer than what you have been used
to than it is to get accustomed to the cold. Even if you have the
appropriate warm clothing, grey and wet winter skies can be
depressing.

> "I was careful to keep warm and not fall sick. I bought
> extra blankets, drank hot tea and bought a humidifier
> and portable heater!"—RF, a Singaporean in Canada

> "I did not adapt very well to the colder climate. My
> heater was on non-stop!"
> —CL, a Singaporean in New Zealand

In a place like Canada, when daylight hours are drastically
shortened in the winter, scientists have discovered that the lack
of sunshine affects a person's mood. That aside, if you are properly dressed, it will go a long way towards helping you to see the
winter through without succumbing to depression and ill health.
Warm winter clothing is not a luxury. You need it in order to
stay healthy.

Getting yourself exposed to below-freezing temperatures can lead to hypothermia. The handbook that is put out by the Canadian Bureau for International Education warns foreign students to get into the habit of listening to the weather forecast on the local radio station at the beginning of the day and to dress accordingly.

PROBLEMS OF DISCRIMINATION

One fear a foreign student may have is that of being a target of racism and discrimination. It is unavoidable that you will feel different in terms of your nationality, ethnic background, religion and customs.

It is possible that you will experience very generalised instances of racism—for instance, graffiti attacking a particular race—but actual racial attacks are rare on university campuses. Sometimes, you may read about foreign students being blamed for taking up limited places in universities that should have gone to the local student population, so there may be agitation for more rigorous language proficiency tests or for foreign student fees to be raised even higher.

If you have an unpleasant encounter with a native of the country, you should ask yourself if the unpleasantness was the direct result of racial or ethnic discrimination, as there is no denying that where many cultures meet, there is likely to be such incidences. However, most foreign students have not experienced these themselves, although almost everyone has a story to relate of somebody who has been a victim.

If you are worried about being the target of such discrimination, it is best to remember that while there are some people who will be prejudiced and you may run into them, there are fewer such people than in the past and there are many more who are not prejudiced and will welcome you into their society.

Do remember that you are a representative of your home country and culture. What you do will contribute towards the

positive or negative impressions that the people you meet will have of your culture in general. But do not be a propagandist or too vocal a defender of your country's culture and policies, accepting with tact and good humour the cultural differences that you encounter. If you behave creditably and respond well even in trying situations, you can only make it easier for those foreign students who come after you.

Here are some other thoughts on the subject of fitting in:

> *"Keep an open mind. Don't get into discussions about which country is better or worse. Discuss instead the benefits of both countries if you can. People are sensitive and patriotic."*—ZQ, a Canadian in England

> *"Be tolerant. Understand that you chose to be in a*

different culture where teaching and studying habits may not make as much sense as you'd like, but that's the way things are and do not be overly critical. Balance studies with play. After all, learning doesn't just take place inside the classroom."

—*YP, an American in Japan*

Chapter Seven

STUDENT LIFE

Now you are really on your own. You experience such a sense of independence, free of Mum's apron strings. There is nobody around to tell you what to do. But with this independence comes the weight of responsibility and the need to make really important decisions. You will also find that the business of daily living can be quite tedious and time-consuming, taking away a lot of precious hours that can be spent with your books.

MAKING YOUR DOLLAR STRETCH
Gone are the days when the only thing you needed to do to have some money was go to Mum or Dad with your hand outstretched. It may have been a student loan that made your studies abroad possible, or your parents who helped you on your

educational journey. Now, you find that you have X number of dollars—and it is your duty to BUDGET!

Budgeting strategies can take many forms, from the very minimalist to the most detailed accounting. A person who is habitually frugal may find little difficulty in spending within his or her means, or even have a little left over at the end of the month for some special treats. But for the not-so-organised, this part of student life can have many pitfalls.

Much of the time, though, common sense and a responsible attitude will prevail and see most students through. Many of them do not have a system or method of budgeting but try their best to be thrifty, and this is often good enough.

> *"I had no budget, but I should have had one. I've basically just spent far too much!"*
>   —*KW, a Briton in Canada*

> *"I was given a set amount by my parents every year. I paid the essentials when due, and set aside pocket money. Any unused portion was placed in a short-term fixed deposit."—DP, a Singaporean who was in Australia*

> *"When I stayed with my relatives, my main expenses were petrol for my car and food when I ate out, so budgeting was relatively easy. When I moved out ... wow, I then realised how expensive it could get. All the little things do add up. Solution ... buy in bulk!"*
>   —*CCY, a Singaporean who studied in the US*

> *"I kept a record book."—CL, a Singaporean who was in New Zealand*

> *"I'm frugal."—ZQ, a Canadian who studied in the United Kingdom*

Most universities and colleges will provide a very general guideline on how much you can expect to pay for course fees, books and accommodation. If you are living on campus or with a family, your meals are often a part of the overall arrangement, and this simplifies matters. Even so, it is best if you know exactly how much money you have to spend as it is good to have some general sense of what your major expenses will be. Apart from course fees and books, there will be the cost of accommodation (renting on- or off-campus, or a homestay arrangement), food, utilities, transport and clothing.

Telephone bills can take a big chunk out of your allowance as long-distance calls home are a costly affair. Take note that there are certain times during the day and night when it is more economical for you to make an international call, and that phone companies may have special plans that offer savings on phone numbers that you call frequently. Anything left over can then be spent on a little entertainment for yourself, like going to the movies or having a meal out.

MONEY MANAGEMENT TIPS

First of all, you will need to establish a bank account in your name. Most of you will have had sufficient experience in opening and handling a bank account. Those who are not so familiar with this necessary financial aspect of modern living will probably have parents or guardians who will accompany you on your first trip to your host country and set up an account for you. It will be a good move for you to find a bank that has branches in both your home country and your new one as that would facilitate banking queries and transactions, but there is no cause for concern if this is not possible. Most banks have no problems dealing with foreign banks. Make an appointment with a bank official, who will be able to advise you on the best and most efficient means of making sure that you have money remitted regularly into your account.

It is important to work out a budget. Before going abroad, you should sit and work out how much you need for various items—tuition fees and books, accommodation, food, utilities, clothing, transport and entertainment, among others (See Chapter Four for tips on how to do this). You will probably go through this exercise with your parent, on whom you are likely to depend for financial support during your studies abroad. By doing this, you will be able to work out your budget for a specific period—say, a semester of so many months.

Now that you have a budget, the second step is to determine exactly how much you spend on each item, as and when you spend it. However, most students do not have much of a budgeting and spending strategy as their time is taken up with studies, so you will want to do this in the easiest way possible. One method is to have a series of envelopes into which you put the apportioned amount of money for each type of expenditure. Then when you get a heating bill, for example, pay for it with money from the utilities envelope and replace it with the bill or receipt. After a few months, you will be able to determine if your initial budget was a realistic one or not.

If you find that your food envelope is consistently empty before the end of the month, it will be relatively easy for you to check on how you have been spending the food money if you have kept the receipts in one envelope. That will help you decide whether you have been too extravagant, perhaps eating out far too often instead of cooking for yourself. An adjustment in spending habits may be necessary or, perhaps, a call home to your parents with a well-founded argument on why your allowance should be increased.

> "No, I did not have a budget. My parents gave me a specific amount to spend in each semester and, by the time I had spent on the essentials, there was very often very little left over. I frequently went months without

*having any extra money to spend on luxuries like going
to the movies."—CC, a Singaporean in Canada*

YOUR HOME AWAY FROM HOME

If your course of study is not too long, say, within a year, living
in a hostel or dormitory on campus or with a local family is your
best option. Sometimes, staying with a host family may be your
only choice at the start of your study abroad if the college or
university does not have any on-campus accommodation. These
arrangements are often made at the time when you apply for
your course of study, before you leave home. They can be made
through your university or through the agent handling your
application to study abroad.

The advantage of living with a host family is that you get an
opportunity to immerse yourself in the culture of the country
you are in. This is an important consideration, especially for
students who are on an exchange programme, because one main
reason why such students go on exchange programmes is to
learn at first hand how people in other cultures live.

*"My homestay family had three daughters, the youngest
of whom was my age. I got along with the entire family
very well. Although they didn't speak much English,
they were very nice and made me feel welcome, which
helped greatly with my settling in a new country. I had
most of my evening meals with them and they tried to
include me in as many of their activities as possible. I
was given my own room with all the necessities in it, so
there wasn't much need for me to buy anything to make
the room liveable."*

—YP, an American who was in Japan

But what is an advantage can also become a bad experience if
you are ill-prepared to adjust to a different lifestyle. If you are

used to a more modern and westernised way of life, for example, being thrown into a very traditional, Japanese style of living is a great cultural shock. You may find your room tiny and cramped by comparison, and discover that you have given up your comfortable bed at home for a *futon* on a *tatami* mat. No steak and potatoes or apple pies here. Instead, you get rice in a bowl with chopsticks, with accompanying dishes of noodles, seaweed, *tofu* and the like.

It is really important, therefore, to make sure that you are mentally prepared for the challenges that living with a host family will pose to you.

> *"It took me about four months to really belong to the family. I had problems with the different food, lifestyle, cold weather and the dog in the family! Even daily stuff like doing the dishes and laundry were different."*
> —CLT, *a Singaporean in Canada*

Prepare yourself for the different cultural experience and, above all, have a positive attitude and a willingness to accept what may be very different from what you have been used to so far.

Sometimes, the family you are with turns out to be a poor host. Some students have returned with stories about how badly they were treated, how disinterested the host family was in their welfare and in communicating with them, and how living conditions were so uncomfortable.

Accommodation in a campus residence will usually provide you with more privacy and freedom of movement as you do not develop a sense of intrusion into someone else's home. Universities offer all manner of residences, from dormitories with single rooms you can have to yourself, or double rooms that have to be shared with a roommate, to self-contained apartments for married students.

Rules and regulations in university residences vary greatly, not only from university to university but even among residences in the same campus. But you should expect that there may be restrictions regarding visitors, noise levels, special considerations during examination times, and so on.

Despite the restrictions, however, accommodation in an on-campus residence may well be an easier option—unless you are interested in a cultural experience as mentioned earlier—as there are fewer adjustments you will have to make. There is also the convenience of having everything that you need close by. Lectures, tutorials, university functions and fellow students are all near you. Most campuses also have many food outlets, bookshops and convenience services like a laundromat or post office. If you so desire, you can spend all your years at university without ever leaving the campus grounds!

> *"I lived on campus. It was a lot more convenient. There was no need for commuting and it helped me to meet other students. Night classes were not a problem. However, one does get sick of being 'in school' every single day, and it took me longer to find my way around the city."—CLT, a Singaporean in Canada*

Given all this, why would anyone want to choose to live away from the campus? Sometimes there is no on-campus accommodation available, or you may want to look for your own accommodation only after having lived on campus for a while. It will probably be too expensive to do on your own, so this is likely to be the result of having found some friends with whom you think you can get along famously. If you are lucky enough to have a group with whom to share an apartment, it will prove to be an even more economical arrangement that will also allow you greater freedom so that you can have a "home away from home".

"I lived on campus for the first semester because it was compulsory. After that, I lived off campus with another Singaporean, because I didn't like the dorm."
—*LSY, a Singaporean who was in the United States*

Your campus friends are probably your best sources of information on where you can find affordable housing and what rental rates are like. Bulletin boards on campus, advertisements in the newspapers and real estate agents who deal in rentals are other sources of information. Often, you can take over a rental from students who are finishing their study term but take this route very cautiously. There are many pitfalls that can spell disaster. You may have to provide your own household items like linen, dishes and cooking utensils. There are rights and responsibilities that the landlord and you, as a tenant, should know about. Make sure you do not sign a lease until you have fully understood all the conditions.

LIVING TOGETHER
Speaking of pitfalls, one of the greatest lies in the selection of the person you share your living quarters with. There is a big difference between friends and roommates or flatmates. You do not have to live with your friends, but a roommate is someone you share much of your space with, both physically and mentally.

"If you get a roommate who doesn't do anything, you're like a live-in maid. You have to be able to get along."
—*SS, a Singaporean in Canada*

"Living with roommates is like losing most of your privacy, especially when the two of you are not close but don't hate each other!"—*SB, an Indonesian in Canada*

Think about your personal habits. Are you a very tidy person

103

who does not like to have things out of place? Do you take your shoes off before entering your home? Can you cook, and are you used to a kitchen where everything is where it should be and dishes are washed after every meal? Do you like to keep your toothbrush in its place and the bath always scrubbed clean as a pin? Do you like to sleep early and rise early in the day?

Let us assume the answer is "yes" to all these questions, and then contrast such a person with one who is the very opposite. This would be someone who walks all over the carpet with shoes on, even though they may be dirty; who cannot tell the salt from the sugar; leaves the dirty dishes in the kitchen sink until there is nothing clean left in the cupboard; leaves the soap melting in a pool of water and hair clogging the drain; loves to play loud music and really comes to life only after midnight, and so on.

> *"I couldn't believe how one person could wreak such havoc on the place. When she finished cooking, there was sauce all over the walls, and she clogged up the bathtub so that the water couldn't drain properly. Worse of all, when I was studying for my finals, she invited her friends over, making so much noise that I was driven to distraction."—DR, a Singaporean in Canada*

Rooming together works best if you know your companions fairly well and, even so, there must be a lot of give and take. A foursome, for example, made things work for them. They were a brother and sister pair who were friends with two cousins. They worked out a kitchen roster, each taking turns to cook and wash up. They went shopping for groceries in a group and split the rent, food and utility bills evenly four ways. Three years of living together and looking after each other, especially during difficult times like bouts of illnesses and examination periods, knitted them into a little family group. There were personal frictions but these were overlooked in favour of the general good.

> *"Everybody has a different lifestyle. You have to get used to that. Be considerate and air any differences out in the open."—CLT, a Singaporean in Canada*

> *"You have to respect others, but don't let people walk over you. If you have a cleaning schedule, then everybody must follow it, otherwise no one will."*
> *—AJ, a Swede in Canada*

FOOD, GLORIOUS FOOD!

Some parts of this topic have been covered incidentally in the discussions on where to stay. If it is a taste of true local fare that you want, there is nothing to beat the experience of living with a host family and sharing their meals. This can be an exciting or difficult experience, depending on how open you are to new experiences and how willing you are to stretch your taste buds to new limits.

> *"Food was less of a problem than I had imagined. There were a lot of choices outside of eating sushi and sashimi every day, and many reasonably priced eateries could be*

found near the campus. Those were the places where my friends and I found lunch every day. ... Although Tokyo was generally expensive, if we looked hard enough, we could find restaurants that were quite affordable."
— *YP, an American in Japan*

Food in halls of residence is safe and plentiful, but often boring. Those who have had to endure three years or more of such fare often have but one word to describe it—"horrible".

Respite from daily assaults on one's taste and sensibilities, however, can be found quite easily. As most universities are located in fairly large and cosmopolitan cities, you should be able to find some places serving the kind of food that you are used to—Chinese, Indian, Greek, Italian, Mexican and so on. Then there is always the fast food variety—the burgers and fries that anyone will find comfortingly familiar. The larger campuses will have an assortment of coffee houses, café and restaurants.

Sometimes, a yearning for something home-cooked can be so strong as to inspire simple but creative solutions. A student who lived in an Australian university hostel missed her Chinese *congee* and noodles so much that she bought an electric rice cooker and cooked more than rice in it. Of course, she had to keep her window wide open to make sure that the cooking odours were not detected as cooking in the rooms was not permitted.

> "My biggest problem was just finding a supermarket at first as I didn't know which bus to get on. I brought a few cooking implements with me and bought a few more here."—KW, a Briton in Canada

The best arrangement is definitely one in which you are able to do your own cooking. Do check with the university administration on whether there are some hostels that allow such an arrangement. If you are able to cook, you can be assured that as long as you are in a big city, whether it is San Francisco, London, Montreal, Melbourne or Wellington, you will be able to get all the special ethnic ingredients that are required for you to cook up a storm.

STUDY SKILLS AND TIME MANAGEMENT

Whether you have decided on continuing your education after having been out in the workplace for a while or are fresh from school, you can be sure of this: your studying skills and determination to succeed will be severely tested.

Above all, these years as a foreign student will require organisation, discipline and much hard work. It helps if you are naturally organised and systematic in everything you do. Always organise some plan for your studying, but remember that plans should always be revised because it is difficult to come up with a plan that works perfectly all the time.

Developing a daily schedule that covers all the things you have to do each day may be a little too rigid for many people. What you can do is to work out a schedule on a weekly basis together with an overall schedule reminding you of the bigger picture—when assignments are due, examination dates and deadlines, for example.

☛ *The goal is to apportion your time so that you will be able to fit in all the essentials—you must have time to attend classes, study, eat and sleep. There will be the necessary chores like cooking, doing your laundry and shopping, and you must have some time for recreation and socialising.*

Drawing up a "to do" list will help you keep track of daily tasks and give you a feeling of control. It will help you to enforce self-discipline, something you will need a lot of because, being overseas, there will be no one to see to it that you get your work done except yourself. With organisation and discipline, you will ensure that you keep your studies under control and that it is not taking over your entire life. You have to control the work or the work will control you.

> *"Start work right away! It is easier to take time off later than to try and catch up."*—AJ, a Swede in Canada

> *"My advice is to get to know your professors on a one-to-one basis by seeing them after class, during office hours. And keep up with course work."*
> —CLT, a Singaporean in Canada

In addition to these essentials, it will be useful for you to hone specific study skills such as learning how to listen carefully during lectures and tutorials, how to filter the information you have acquired and how to apply it (in essays, tests and examina-

108

tions). There are many books written on the subject and it will be a good idea to read some of them.

Your college or university may occasionally organise seminars or courses on study skills. Do not ignore the help that these can offer as it is far better to seek any assistance you can in this new learning environment than wait until late in the academic year when you may have to hit the panic button.

INTERNSHIPS

Many colleges and universities provide students, both undergraduates and graduate students, with an opportunity to work in their area of study and to earn credits for it. Sometimes, you can even get paid for the work, although you may run into some visa problems if this is the case. You should check such details with the university or the host country's embassy before starting out if you are planning to enrol in cooperative or internship programmes.

Such programmes are available in an increasing number of disciplines. In some fields of study and in certain universities, they may even be a mandatory part of the course. For example, an engineering student may, after the first year of study, have to work for a period of time with an engineering firm before continuing with academic work. If you are accepted into an internship programme, your university will usually be the one to provide you with the opportunity to go into a specific workplace. However, you will still have to go through an interview process and you should be aware that, in some programmes, not all the students are always able to be placed. On the job, you will be supervised by your professor as well as by the supervisor who is your employer or superior in the business where you are working.

Such a working experience will give you the opportunity to practise what you have learned in the classroom. It has an added advantage of giving you a taste of what working in your discipline will be like once you have finished your studies, so that you will know if it is what you really want to do.

STUDENT SUPPORT SERVICES

Most universities which have a large international student population have special support services like an international student counsellor. When you are enrolled in a college or university, you should have received information about the facilities that are available and whether or not there is such a counsellor or office that provides support services to foreign students.

The office will probably provide special facilities for different nationality and religious groups—for instance, a non-denominational prayer room—and organise functions to celebrate different cultural events. It would be one place where you can be in touch with other students from your own country and build up a support system.

The counsellor is someone whom you can talk to and who has been trained to listen to your problems while keeping in mind that you come from a different cultural background. Through the office of the student counsellor, the college or university provides counselling sessions, talks and workshops on how to cope with the problems of being a foreign student.

As a foreign student, you may have other problems apart from your studies. There will be adjustments to the new educational system, perhaps language difficulties, perceptions of discrimination and feelings of loneliness and homesickness.

Financial worries are common. You may worry about the expense that your sponsor or family is incurring in supporting your studies. This will put greater pressure on you to succeed and you may suffer from a terrible fear of failure. Some foreign students, bearing this in mind, may cram their courses and take on more than they can handle in order to try and earn their degree or diploma in as short a time as possible. Sometimes, students feel forced to take a course that they really would not like to study because it is what their family—who may have to make sacrifices in order to support their study—wants.

However, most universities are very accommodating when it comes to minor financial problems and if you find yourself faced with a shortage of money at any time, your first step should be to go and discuss it with the university's financial aid office, which can often come up with schemes to cover a short-term financial shortfall—a great stress reliever!

If the foreign student is from a culture in which the need to have counselling or psychiatric services is stigmatised and associated with a loss of "face" or status, he or she may not want to seek the counsellor for advice. However, most universities provide a student health clinic in which fully confidential psychological and psychiatric services are readily available, and you should not feel in any way unusual if you choose to take advantage of these. You will be surprised to find out how many of your fellow students who seem quite "normal" to you are doing so as well! However, such problems, when they are severe and not attended to, often show themselves up in physical ways—thus, the student may have to visit the doctor instead and seek medical attention for symptoms like headaches, stomach upsets, tiredness or general pain.

YOUR SOCIAL LIFE

If you are fairly well organised and manage your time well and, therefore, have some time left to enjoy, your years of study overseas should give you new and rewarding experiences.

If you are one of those students who go abroad with just one goal in mind—to concentrate on your studies—and you choose not to socialise much, that is fine. However, if you would rather not spend your free time alone but your social life is so quiet that one of its highlights is to have a conversation about the weather with the person next to you at the laundromat, you should do something about it. The opportunities are all there.

Whatever your interests, you will find that there will be an outlet for it at the college or university you plan to attend. If you are an active member of your church at home, there will be Christian fellowship gatherings. If you are looking for a new interest, like taking up martial arts, there will probably be a *karate* or *taekwondo* society you can join.

☛ ***Try to find some things to interest you early in your new student life. The more effort and energy you put into it, the greater the returns and enjoyment you will receive.***

Try to make the best use of the social and recreational facilities on campus. There are plenty of catalogues, bulletins and handbooks that will tell you what is available. You can join all sorts of recreational activities and sports such as tennis, soccer and football; musical groups like bands and choirs; social and debating clubs; and service and religious organisations. There will also be an active ongoing social calendar of concerts, recitals, plays, dances, films and talks to attend. When there are local festivals, social clubs will organise dinners and dances and other functions to celebrate.

> *"Unfortunately, I spent too much time working to do all that much partying, but the occasional party was fun! The opportunity to party is always there, even if you don't always take it."—KW*

> *"There were get-togethers—dinners, parties, pub crawls—once every two weeks. I played soccer and had practices or games three times a week."—ZQ*

> *"There were lots of extracurricular activities. I joined the photo club, life drawing club and swim club."—AJ*

"There were some parties. Pubs were the norm. I didn't get drunk, which was an exception."—DP

"I watched a lot of movies. I went bowling, biking and skiing. I did not go to many parties as, officially, I was underaged to go to discos. You had to be 21 years old."—CCY

"The favourite activity of most of the exchange students was going to the discos. We found cheap ones that catered more to a younger crowd and often spent Fridays or Saturday evenings there."—YP

"I wanted to do something totally different, to get away from my books. Working in the university library till late at night meant that I often travelled home after dark, so I decided to attend the karate lessons. By the time I got my degree, I was a much fitter person and, even though I did not get any brown or black belt, I think I can defend myself quite confidently against an attacker."—BR

VACATIONS

Apart from social activities that are available on campus, you should try to do a little travelling and see a bit of the country you are in during the few breaks from studies that you get during the year.

Many foreign students simply focus on getting a degree as quickly as they can and going home. This is understandable considering the financial burden their families are bearing on their account. Some universities have their courses and semesters structured in such a way that, if you really want to, you can study all year round and get your degree in half the time that it normally takes.

But, money and time permitting, do try to fit in a bit of travelling during your stint overseas or you may regret not having made use of the opportunity.

☞   *Bear in mind that as a student, you may be able to get special student rates from travel and tour companies. It is always worth asking. But make sure that you go to a reputable travel agent.*

If you are travelling out of the country, check with immigration authorities or the foreign student adviser on the requirements for re-entry into the country before you leave. If you had needed a visitor's visa when you first arrived, it may be necessary to obtain a new one when you return from your vacation.

Many students go home if they and their families can afford the cost of the trip. Their responses to these visits home vary. For some, after months of wrestling with homesickness while trying to get good grades and making sure that there are clean socks to wear, it feels good to be pampered and to have all the creature comforts of home and family life, and to renew friendships.

> *"The first and last part of my vacations are always interesting and exciting. I tend to meet all my friends and family when I first arrive and again during the last two weeks of my holiday to say goodbye. The middle part of my vacation can be rather dull because most of my friends are busy, either in school or with work."*
>
> *TW, a Singaporean in Canada*

Depending upon your temperament, however, the comforts of home and family can be restrictive. Living away from home has taught you the values of independence and self-sufficiency. You have had to make decisions on your own every day, often with no one to consult, affecting no one but yourself. Your lifestyle has possibly changed quite drastically and you eat, sleep and study when you please. But back home again, the pleasures of not having to cook and clean up are offset by having your freedom curtailed somewhat.

> *"Visits home were enjoyable but stressful. It was difficult at first coping with changes in the country and having to get used to being at home with the family again. It was a little restrictive, but you knew it was temporary."*
> —CL, a Singaporean in New Zealand

> *"I found it very hot and humid, and I had to re-adjustments. It was very boring because four months is very long without any work or school. Of course, I had lots of local food!."*—CLT, a Singaporean in Canada

SUMMER JOBS

For many local students, summer is a time to gain temporary employment that will help them to supplement the allowance that they get from home. Some societies recognise that many students, both local and foreign, depend upon what they can earn working part-time to help pay for their education, and that working during vacations is an important part of student life. Many businesses are prepared to employ students just for the summer. Students can find employment in all kinds of jobs as cashiers, waiters or waitresses, pump attendants and sales people.

Some countries, however, do not allow foreign students to be employed while they hold a student's visa. When this is the case, they are generally very strict about the rule and will not allow a foreign student to work even part-time or do casual work like babysitting. An exception may be made if your employment is a part of your study programme, or if it is a teaching or research assistantship or fellowship.

Sometimes, if circumstances beyond your control make it

necessary for you to work for extra income, as in a case where your sponsor or family is unable to continue providing for your education, a special case may be made, and an employment authorisation issued to you.

☛   *Make sure you check with the government authority or the university staff before you get a job. If you violate your student status, intentionally or otherwise, it may result in your stay in the country being terminated.*

Chapter Eight

RETURNING HOME

When you first arrived in the country, you experi[enced]
shock because you had to adjust to a new environ[ment]
extremely anxious because you did not know how [to]
adapt. You were lonely and homesick, and burde[ned]
of failure.

After some time, however, your fears were a[llayed]
settled into the rhythm of your new, indep[endent]
became confident, made new friends and met [new]
college life, finally emerging with the desired [degree]
in your hand.

Now that it is almost time to return ho[me]
that you will feel the wrench of saying go[odbye]
have changed! What were once strange su[rroundings]

117

taken on the familiarity of home. You have made a lot of friends you are loath to say goodbye to. What's more, doubts start to assail you—what are you returning home to? This is when a "reverse culture shock" begins to set in.

> *"I made some good friends in my year of study abroad, and it was hard to say goodbye although I was looking forward to returning home. We comforted ourselves by promising to keep in touch."—YP, American in Japan*

> *"I felt awfully sad and disoriented. I wished I could have stayed on, but family ties brought me back."*
> —*CL, Singaporean in New Zealand*

TOUGH CHOICES

You are approaching the end of your course of study and now, even as you take your final examinations, doubts begin to assail you. You may have gone overseas to study with the idea that, with a degree in hand, you would be equipped with the necessary per qualifications and skills to get a job and earn a reasonably od salary back home. Now, some niggling thoughts are trou- ng you—was the course you took the right one for you, and do u really want to pursue this course of work?. These are two stions that constantly surface. Another question that you asking yourself is whether you have worked hard enough.

Towards the end of your course, you will also have to con- r whether you want to go on to a further and higher course udy, or whether it is time to return home and take up a job. foreign students do return home. If you are one of them verything turns out exactly as you had planned, all is well u. But even if your plans are changed, you should not be ointed. You will recall that, at the beginning of the book, vantages of going abroad to study were discussed. Those ave done it agree wholeheartedly that the experience was well worth any difficulties that they had to overcome. It broadened their minds and made them self-reliant, independent and confident.

The new skills and qualities that you have acquired will now help you to decide if, after all, you should go for a higher degree, change courses or specialise further. You will find that you have just taken but one more step in a lifelong educational trail.

PREPARING FOR YOUR RETURN HOME

When you left home, your travel arrangements were probably made for you by your family. Now, you will have to make your own arrangements. When buying your air ticket, do it through a reputable travel agent. Also, make sure you understand all the rules and regulations concerning luggage, check-in time, what happens if you were to cancel your flight reservation, and the granting of refunds. As a student, you may be eligible for a discount on the airfare and other savings.

If your accommodation is off-campus, you will have to settle affairs with your landlord. You had probably paid a deposit at the beginning of your stay. Check to see if this deposit is to be offset against your last month's rent, or if it is to be refunded, provided there has been no damage to the apartment during the course of your stay. Your terms of agreement may require you to give the premises a thorough cleaning before handing it over to the landlord.

With regard to your course of study, after the results of the final examinations are released, there will be a time lapse before the convocation ceremony. Some students remain for this largely ceremonial proceeding, while others are anxious to return home. Your attendance at the convocation ceremony is seldom compulsory, but it is a fitting and satisfying end to the hard work that you have put into your study over the years and is especially meaningful if your family is able to come and share this experience of graduating with you.

Whether or not you are at the convocation, make sure that all the paperwork with the college or university authorities is cleared—that any tuition fees and outstanding payments are settled—so that you will receive your academic transcripts and certificate, diploma or degree.

THOSE PACKING BLUES

Remember those two suitcases you came with? Over time, they have expanded into a whole room or apartment full of your personal possessions. Now, you are faced with the task of finding some way to organise it all in time for your return home. If you are lucky, you may have someone—a relative, for example, who will store your things for you until you can arrange to get them back.

> *"I had help. My things were stored with relatives and returned to me piecemeal every time someone visited the country."*—DP, *Singaporean in Australia*

You will probably just want to bring home your personal belongings, clothes and books. If you have any electronic equipment, like stereo equipment or a computer, you will have to weigh the pros and cons of taking them home or leaving them behind. Should you decide to take them along, check that they will actually work back home! Unless you are really attached to such items, you may want to sell them for the best price you can get. It is a lot of trouble to ensure that such delicate items are packed very carefully so that they arrive undamaged. Pass the word around early, and put up advertisements on student bulletin boards and campus newspapers.

> *"I arranged for my trunk and other items to be packed and shipped back. I paid all my bills, but did not close my savings account, which I should have done. Clothes that I didn't want to take home were given to the Salvation Army and I arranged for a friend to drive me to the airport."*—LSY, Singaporean in the United States

A shipping company will get your boxes on a ship, but will not do the crating for you without extra charge. Consider, too, whether your goods require any insurance. Wherever it is you are shipping from and to whichever country, you should allow at least a month for the shipment to reach its destination. When your boxes arrive home, it is important to get them out of the company's warehouse as soon as possible. You are normally given a few days' grace, because you will usually have to clear them through the customs yourself, after which you will have to pay extra for each additional day of storage.

STAYING IN TOUCH

Just as you did when you first left home, you will want to keep in touch with the people you are now leaving behind—mainly, your college and university friends. The end of the academic year can be a hectic time during which you will have to deal with sitting for your final examinations while preparing for your return home at the same time. In the midst of all this, do not forget to get the addresses and telephone numbers of your friends, because there is a tendency after the exams for everyone to go their separate ways very quickly.

> *"Ensure you maintain contact with your new friends once you return, otherwise the benefits of contacts are lost."—DP*

> *"I was a little sad but glad to go home. I went round the university taking pictures and saying goodbye to my professors and friends."—LSY*

Some universities try to keep in touch with alumni who have returned home. As a returned foreign student, you can be of enormous help in recruitment programmes and in providing future foreign students from your country with orientation prior to their departure.

REJOINING THE FAMILY

This can be a very difficult adjustment to make. When you first return home, you may experience a sense of elation, having achieved what you set out to do. Naturally, you will be eager to return to your family and friends but, at some point, you will realise that your home environment has changed. At first, you will have everyone's attention. But after a while, those at home will be tired of hearing about your experience abroad—and often much quicker than you tire of telling them about it!

Moreover, during the time you were abroad, you were also growing older and more mature. You learned to manage on your own, and had to make decisions without the benefit of family advice. Your decisions and actions had no bearing on anyone else except yourself. Now, you have to re-learn the skills of living together. Your family will also have to adjust to the fact that the young person who left home a year or more ago is, in many ways, not the same person as the one who has now returned, and that his or her outlook on life may have changed substantially. Parents must also learn to let go a little and be prepared to welcome home a young adult.

> *"I had to get used to living in a family unit again, and others to consider with regard to meals and family outings. I left as a child, but came back as a working adult. This was trying."—BR, Singaporean in Canada*

FITTING BACK INTO THE CULTURE

If you have been studying in a country that is culturally different from your own, you will find that you experience culture shock not once, but twice—when you first entered that new culture, and again when you return to your own. In some ways, this "reverse culture shock" is more startling because you would hardly expect to feel uncomfortable or strange in your own country. Yet, consider this. You have spent most of your time in a university concerned mainly with your studies and not much more. This is an artificial environment, being in an "ivory tower". Returning home now throws you back into the real world.

You will see everything with new eyes. Dirty streets, poverty and unsanitary habits that you had never noticed before or took for granted now offend your new sensibilities. On the other hand, many improvements may have taken place—such as new buildings and better roads—while you were away.

These physical differences will be the first you will notice, but they are also easier to readjust to. Less obvious are the subtle cultural differences. You may find that you no longer share the value system that is prevalent in your own country. The freedom you experienced in debating ideas and expressing your opinion during your years as a student abroad may have to be curbed in a society where saving face is important and authority always has to be deferred to.

Those whose time abroad was short—perhaps they were students on a cultural exchange or postgraduate course that lasted a year or less—will naturally experience reverse culture shock to a lesser degree. But even they will now reflect and think differently about themselves and their own culture, having developed new insights as a result of the new perspective they have gained.

☛ *The bottom line for any returning student is to be aware of how you have changed and how this impacts on those around you. Also, be tolerant of people who take a lot longer to adjust to these changes than you think they should!*

THE LAST WORD

Finally, here are what some students have to say about their experience to someone like you who is contemplating going abroad. No matter how they put it, the verdict is: Go for it!

> *"Enjoy it. Always stay active with sports and participate in the local pastimes. Respect etiquette. Bring back the things that are important to you, especially addresses."*
> —RDS, who was in Germany

> *"It's a very good experience since it forces you to grow up to be more independent. But be sure that you are here to study, not to have fun. So even when you have lots of freedom, don't get too carried away and don't expect that your life in a foreign country will be 'enjoyable' in the sense that you should not expect yourself to be living like you used to at home."*—SB, who is in Canada

"Know what you want to do and stick to it, because there are so many possibilities that it can get very intimidating. If I had to do it again, I would do things differently. I would explore my educational avenues and not let anyone influence or confuse me."—CC, who is in Canada

"I would do it again. I feel the experience has made me more in touch with myself and more independent. During my time abroad, I enjoyed meeting people in another country and getting to know their way of life. I felt I understood what it meant to be British and saw the world through the eyes of students in the UK. It surprised me how different their perceptions and culture were. Most important of all, going to England made me appreciate Canada and Canadians. I now love the sight of each pine tree, the mountains, the wide roads, the bigger cars, the new store fronts, the bilingual labels, the hockey, the snow, and so on. I also feel closer to my friends and family. I appreciate them more."
                    —ZQ, who was in the United Kingdom

"I would definitely recommend going abroad to study. It's an experience I will always treasure. Especially if one is studying a language, I think there is no better way to learn than to be in the country where it's spoken. As a student, that one year or few years abroad is not going to be the same as if you were going to work there. I think the level of enjoyment for learning about a new culture is much greater. You don't have the same pressures knowing that it's only temporary. I would do it all over again."—YP, who was in Japan

"Definitely, I'd recommend going abroad. Yes, I would do it again. I'd be more interactive with the Japanese

and assimilate more. It was fun as the year really opened me up. It gave me a wider perspective than just studying."—DP, who was in Japan

"Going abroad can only be a good thing. If nothing else, you'll be more independent and you'll also probably gain a wealth of experience and meet loads of interesting people. You may be scared to study abroad, but I'll bet that by the time you reach the end of your study, you will not want to go home!"—KW, who is in Canada

Appendix

HOW DO I FIND OUT MORE?

PART ONE—GLOSSARY

A. Useful institutional definitions

University An academic institution that grants undergraduate and graduate degrees in a variety of fields and that supports degree-granting professional schools which are not exclusively technological (such as medicine, education or law). Programmes are academically based and usually four years in duration. Universities are often composed of a number of "schools" or "colleges", each of which encompasses several general fields of study.

College An institution which offers educational instruction beyond the secondary school level, usually granting diplomas rather than degrees (except in the United States). Programmes are skill-based, often involving some form of specialist vocational training, and range from two to four years in duration.

Junior college (US only) An institution offering either the first two years of a four-year university degree, with onward transfer to a university at the end of this time, or providing specialist two-year courses culminating in either a two-year associate degree or a diploma.

Engineering or technical college An independent professional school (public or private) which provides training programmes in the fields of engineering or the physical sciences.

Military academy Military academies are universities run by national governments for the express purpose of preparing officers for the army, navy and air force. Depending on the country, candidates nearly always have to be citizens of the country concerned, sometimes also having to secure the endorsement of local politicians. They have to agree to serve for a period of time in the armed forces following their graduation. Military colleges usually offer degree programmes in engineering and technology with concentrations in various aspects of military science.

Nursing school There are two kinds of nursing school. At schools affiliated with major teaching hospitals or universities, students take university courses as well as practical training and graduate with nursing degrees as well as nursing certification, while at schools affiliated with colleges, emphasis is placed on the practical side of the training and students receive only the appropriate nursing certification.

Business school Business schools also fall into two categories—those which are part of a university and offer degree programmes in a range of business-related disciplines, and those which offer a wider range of subjects geared to providing quick courses in specific areas tagged to current market demands. There is a wide difference in admission standards and qualifications obtained between these two types of school and they should not be confused.

B. Useful application and admission terms to know

Application form This is the document sent to the applicant for completion and submission to the post-secondary institution being applied to. Application forms vary greatly—some are quite simple and some quite lengthy, depending on how much information the institution considers necessary for it to have to make an informed decision on whether to admit a student. Some application forms require supporting materials, such as a personal essay from the applicant, and nearly all ask for a transcript to be submitted in support of the application.

Common application form Sometimes a group of universities or colleges—or even all the post-secondary institutions in a particular region or country—that have agreed upon a common application procedure will have established a centre for the processing of applications to which all applications for these institutions must be sent. This usually allows the applicant to apply to more than one institution using the same application form.

Transcript An official document issued by the secondary school or university you last attended, containing a complete record of the marks obtained in all courses taken at that institution, This is usually sent directly from the sending institution to the one to which you are applying and has to be officially certified as correct and unaltered.

Letter of reference This can be either an overview of your academic achievements to date or a comment on your personal suitability as a candidate for admission to the institution requesting it. Not all post-secondary institutions require these but many do, and they usually want them to be sent directly by the referee to the institution concerned. This is to make sure that they are accurate and unbiased.

Notification date This is the earliest date at which the institution to which you have applied will let you know whether you have been accepted or not. This is sometimes set by the institution itself and sometimes by the government controlling the university. Sometimes, a common notification date has been set, before which no institution under that jurisdiction is allowed to make an offer of admission.

Rolling admissions Usually used only by American universities, a rolling admission policy allows a college to make a decision on an application for admission at any time of the year as soon as all the materials required have been submitted and without waiting for any specific notification date.

Early decision This allows a particularly well-qualified student an opportunity to receive an early answer on admission without waiting for the final completion of his or her application qualifications. Early decision can usually be requested from only one post-secondary institution and, if granted, is considered as binding, with the student having to withdraw all other active applications.

C. Terms commonly used at universities

Freshman A first-year undergraduate student.

Sophomore A second-year undergraduate student.

Junior A student in his or her third undergraduate year.

Senior A graduating undergraduate student in a final year.

Upperclassman Any undergraduate student not in his or her first year.

Graduate student A student who has finished his or her undergraduate degree and who has returned to university for further study.

Exchange student A student from another country (or sometimes another university in the same country) who is attending the university for a particular reason but will not graduate from there.

Calendar A prospectus put out by an university giving details of admission requirements and courses offered by the faculties in that university.

PART TWO—MATERIALS FOR IMMEDIATE USE

A. Specimen letter requesting information from a university or college anywhere in the world (See next page)

B. The comparative costs of studying overseas
(See Page 133—All figures are approximate and are based on the annual cost for an undergraduate degree, unless otherwise stated)

....
(Your address)
....
(Date)

The Admissions Officer,
Name of University/College
Street/City
State/Country
Postal Code

Dear Admissions Officer,

I am a student at .... and I am interested in
pursuing my current studies to a higher level by attending your institution's ....(name of programme).

I am a .... (nationality) citizen. Please
send me, as soon as possible, general information on
your institution, specific details for .... programme and an application form for admission. I would
also appreciate any information you may have on scholarships and other financial aid provisions designed specifically for overseas students.

I would be grateful if you could despatch this information in the fastest way possible, as there may be delays
in ordinary mail. Thank you for your assistance. I look
forward to hearing from you.

Yours sincerely,

(Name typed, accompanied by signature)

Post-secondary institutions in English-speaking countries

Britain
Tuition fees £6,000-£8,000
Living expenses £3,500
Books and supplies, health insurance and travel costs (depending on personal allowance, location and lifestyle) £5,000

Australia
Tuition fees A$10,000-A$2,000 (arts), A$12,000-A$14,000 (science), A$24,000 (medicine)
Living costs A$10,000-A$12,000 (depending on location)
Books and supplies A$600
Health insurance $150
Travel costs A$1,400
Personal expenses A$3,000

New Zealand
Tuition fees NZ$ 9,000-14, 000
Living costs NZ$8,000
Books and supplies NZ$300-400
Travel costs NZ$800
Personal expenses NZ$2,000

Canada
Tuition fees C$3,000-C$12,000 (depending on university and programme)
Living costs of up to C$10,000 (depending on province and location)
Books and supplies C$800
Health insurance C$250
Travel costs C$1,500
Personal allowance C$3,000

USA
(Figures subject to very wide variations)
Tuition fees US$4,000—US$20,000
Living expenses US$5,000
Books and supplies US$600
Health insurance US$500
Travel costs US$1,200
Personal allowance US$3,000

Post-secondary institutions in non-English-speaking countries

France
(You must speak French and pass a test before you can apply to study there)
Tuition fees French francs 900-1,500
Living expenses French francs 3,600

Germany
(You must speak good German. A fluency test is required and a visa will be issued only if you pass)
Tuition fees are free
Living expenses DM2,000 a month (A bank statement or letter from a guarantor will be required to prove you can afford this!)

Japan
(You should spend at least a year learning Japanese before applying and then you will have to pass a language proficiency test before being granted admission)
Tuition fees ¥550,000-¥690,000
Living expenses ¥150,000

C. Some major universities in selected countries

Australia
Australian National University, Canberra
Bond University, Queensland
Flinders University, South Australia
Griffith University, Queensland
Monash University, Victoria
Royal Melbourne Institute of Technology, Victoria
The University of New South Wales
The University of Queensland
University of Technology, New South Wales

Canada
Memorial University, Newfoundland
Dalhousie University, Nova Scotia
Technical University of Nova Scotia
McGill University, Quebec
Queen's University, Ontario
University of Toronto, Ontario
University of Manitoba
University of Saskatchewan
University of Alberta
University of British Columbia
Simon Fraser University, British Columbia

Britain
University of Aberdeen
Buckingham University
University of Bristol
Cambridge University
University of Durham
University of East Anglia
University of Kent

University of London
University of Nottingham
Oxford University
St Andrew's University
University of Sussex
University of Wales

USA
(Based on difficulty of entry)

Very Highly Competitive
Amherst, Massachussets
Brown, Rhode Island
Columbia, New York
Cornell, New York
Duke, North Carolina
Georgetown, DC
Harvard, Massachussets
Johns Hopkins, Maryland
Massachussets Institute of Technology, Massachussets
Princeton, New Jersey
Rice, Tennessee
Stanford, California
University of Pennsylvania
Yale, Connecticut

Highly Competitive
Bates, Maine
Boston, Massachussets
Carnegie-Mellon, Pennsylvania
Emory, Georgia
Lehigh, Pennsylvania
Rutgers, New Jersey
Texas A and M

Tulane, Louisiana
University of California
University of Virginia
Vassar, New York

Competitive
Austin, Texas
Brigham Young, Utah
Drake University, Iowa
Fordham, New York
Loyola, Maryland
Pepperdine, California
Skidmore, New York
University of Florida
University of Iowa
University of North Carolina
University of Southern California
University of Washington
Valparaiso, Pennsylvania

PART THREE—BOOKS AND OTHER PUBLICATIONS

A substantial number of books are available for the student who wants to investigate universities and institutions of higher learning throughout the world. Most of these books are usually well researched, detailed, comparatively simple to use and up to date, but they are not always easy to find. Although they are usually available from the publishers, they are generally expensive to buy and equally expensive to mail, so the best place to look for them initially is in your local university library, although public libraries may also have a limited selection of such books.

The following bibliography includes a cross-section of different kinds of books and other publications, all of which have some connection to the experience of studying overseas. While many of them might appear similar at first glance, there are different purposes or slants to each of them, and this is explained in the notes on each section.

A. Sources of information about overseas universities, colleges and schools and their admission requirements

The World of Learning 42nd Edition 1992
Available from:
Europa Publications Ltd
18, Bedford Square
London, WC1B 3JN
England

According to the cover publicity, this volume purports to be "the most comprehensive and reliable guide to the academic world available in the English language". It gives details of 26,000 universities, colleges, schools of art and music, libraries, learned societies, research institutes, museums and art galleries—arranged alphabetically by country.

Handbook of World Education 1992
Walter Wickremasinghe, Editor in Chief
Available from:
American Collegiate Service
PO Box 442008
Houston, Texas
USA 77244

Subtitled *A Comparative Guide to Higher Education and Educational Systems of the World,* this book has contributions from over 130 different scholars from around the world and is grouped according to country. For each country, it starts with a background history explaining the relationship of education—from elementary and secondary to post-secondary—with the country, then explains the characteristics of higher education at the undergraduate and graduate levels. It also deals with the main issues and trends concerning education in that country, and provides a bibliography particular to these issues.

International Handbook of Universities 13th Edition
Available from:
The International Association of Universities
1 Rue Miollis
75732 Paris Cedex 15
France

A worldwide handbook, it has 9,000 entries, a guide to these entries and a full description of each university. For each institution, it gives details of the academic year, language of instruction, admission requirements, fees, libraries, special facilities, publications, academic staff and student enrolment.

Study Abroad
Available from:
UNESCO
7, Place de Fontenoy
Paris 75352
France

Probably one of the best and most easily available books on the subject. It is divided into two sections. The first deals with international courses and scholarships, grouped in alphabetical order, of contributing international organisations. The second part provides a country by country listing of similar information with general information about the educational system in each country. Although it is quite expensive, this book should be available in most major bookstores.

Profiles of American Colleges
Available from:
Barron's Educational Services
250 Wireless Boulevard
Hauppauge, New York
USA 11788

This book, which deals exclusively with post-secondary institutions in the United States, gives a state by state listing of academic programmes, faculty, class size, campus safety, admission requirements, tuition fees, financial aid, computer facilities, extracurricular activities and sports. It also ranks the degree of competitiveness in trying to gain admission into each institution, from non-competitive to most competitive.

Lovejoy's College Guide
Available from:
Lovejoy's Educational Guides
Prentice Hall General Reference
15, Columbus Circle
New York, New York
USA 10023

This book deals exclusively with US universities and colleges and contains sections on admissions, financial aid, curriculum and special programmes. The section on institutions lists them state by state with a capsule description of each. There is also a small section on foreign universities—some Canadian and some in Europe. This book is easily found in most major bookstores.

The College Handbook: Foreign Student Supplement
Available from:
The College Board
45, Columbus Avenue
New York, New York
USA 10023

This is a companion volume to a much larger publication from the College Board which lists all colleges and universities in the United States (similar to the previous two listings). However, this volume concentrates particularly on topics which specifically concern a student coming from overseas to study in the USA—choosing a university, application procedures for foreign students, admission requirements, costs and test requirements. This book also lists sources of information and advising centres for US universities located in foreign countries.

Admissions Requirements for International Students at Colleges and Universities in the United States
Available from:
Two Trees Press
P.O. Box 8190-10
Fargo, North Dakota
USA

This book describes the kinds of post-secondary institutions in the United States attended by international students, giving the number currently enrolled in each one and what percentage they are of the total student body. It also lists requirements and considerations for the admission of foreign students, including the score required on the TOEFL test.

The Faculty Directory of Higher Education
Available from:
Gale Research Company
835, Penobscot Building
Detroit, Michigan
USA 48226

A 12-volume subject-classified directory with names, addresses and titles of courses taught by more than 600,000 teaching faculties at more than 3,100 US colleges, universities and community colleges, and at 220 selected Canadian institutions.

University and College Entrance
Available from:
Sheed and Ward Ltd
14, Coopers Row
London EC3N 2BH
England
Compiled by the British University and College Admission Service, this book deals exclusively with British post-secondary institutions and advises on how to choose the place of study most appropriate for each individual course of study, and requirements for getting in. It also gives a profile of all of the institutions that can be applied for through the Admission Service.

B. Sources of information on financial aid

International Scholarship Directory: A Complete Guide to Financial Aid for Study Anywhere in the World
Available from:
Career Press
180, Fifth Avenue
PO Box 34
Hawthorne, New Jersey
USA 07507
An extremely useful book containing a "quick find" index, a field of study index, scholarships and awards listings, helpful publications, career information and a sample form letter requesting application information. The directory also points out that "80% of all applications for funds are misdirected or filled out inappropriately" and that "out of over the 7 billion dollars available from corporations, only 400 million was used, the rest going unclaimed".

Annual Register of Grant Support: a Directory of Funding Sources
Available from:

Reed Reference Publishing Company
121, Chanlon Road
New Providence, New Jersey
USA 07974

This authoritative volume contains information on the monies available from private and corporate sources in North America. It also contains a section on how to organise your own programme planning, proposal writing and budget, and its depth of research is excellent.

Scholarships, Fellowships and Loans: A Guide to Educational-Related Financial Aid Programmes for Students and Professionals
Available from:
Gale Research Inc
835, Penobscot Building
Detroit, Michigan
USA 48226

This book lists 3,300 sources of educationally related financial aid and includes specialty indexes to help pin down the most useful ones in each case. These indexes include one each for vocational goals, fields of study, places of study, legal residence requirements and sponsored scholarships.

Free Money for Foreign Study
Laurie Blum
Available from:
Facts on File
460 Park Avenue South
New York, New York
USA 10016

More than 1,000 grants and scholarships that can help both undergraduate and graduate students finance their study abroad are listed here, by country and subject. It includes the names, addresses and phone numbers of sponsors, individual contact people, deadlines, restrictions and amounts given. Reasonably priced, this book is up to date and available in most major bookstores.

The Grants Register
Available from:
Globe Book Services
Brunel Road, Houndmills
Basingstoke, Hampshire
England RG21 2XS

This is a book intended mainly for students at or above the graduate level and for all who require further professional or advanced vocational training. The kinds of financial assistance listed—from international, national governmental or private agencies—include scholarships; fellowships and research grants; exchange opportunities and travel grants; grants for publication, translation and all kinds of artistic and scientific projects; competitions and prizes, and professional and vocational awards; and special awards for minority groups, refugees and so on.

Peterson's Grants for Graduate Students
Available from:
Peterson's Guides
Princeton, New Jersey
USA

The stated purpose is "to supply graduate students and people contemplating graduate study with a list of organisations to which they can apply for funds to support their research and studies". The book's introduction gives details on how to use the book and the criteria for inclusion, while explaining the grant-seeking process itself. It also discusses the issue of how to convince a potential sponsor and how to write a proposal besides giving a sampling of success rates.

Directory of Financial Aids for Women
Gail Ann Schlacter
Available from:
Reference Service Press
San Carlos Industrial Park
1100, Industrial Road, Suite 9
San Carlos, California
USA 94070

This book contains a list of scholarships, fellowships, grants, awards and internships designated primarily or exclusively for women. It also includes local sources of educational benefits and reference sources of financial aid. This company also publishes similar reference volumes for minorities and the disabled.

C. General books on studying overseas

These are books of general information which deal with the whole process of studying overseas. Each book has a short description of its special area of use, and an indication of where it can be found.

Academic Year Abroad
S.J. Steen (ed.)
Available from:
Institute of International Education
809, United Nations Plaza
New York, New York
USA 10017

This book contains chapters on how to read study-abroad books and how to plan for study abroad. The institutions listed are grouped geographically by country and within each country as well. Information is given about the site, academic year dates, subjects offered, eligibility, costs, housing deadlines and contact names and addresses.

Vacation Study Abroad
Available from:
Institute of International Education
809, United Nations Plaza
New York, New York
USA 10017

An excellent book for a student who wants to combine study of all kinds—from rug hooking to bagpipe playing—with the opportunity to travel. Containing both short and long-term study opportunities all over the world, it is readily available in most major bookstores.

A Glossary of Educational Terms: Usage in Five English-Speaking Countries
W.G Walker, J.E. Mumford, Carolyn Steel
Available from:
University of Queensland Press
St. Lucia, Queensland
Australia

As the preface states, "this book arises from difficulties of communication and the lack of common terminology, or at least of a published glossary of terms to describe functions, procedures and institutions in the countries represented". These five countries are Australia, Canada, Britain, New Zealand and the United States. It is a specialised book, sometimes quite hard to find and dated, but it offers excellent help to those who are mystified by the bewildering range of differing academic terms.

Who offers Part-Time Degree Programmes?
Karen C. Hegener (ed.)
Available from:
Peterson's Guides
Princeton, New Jersey
USA

This book gives a description of courses available at US universities on a part-time, evening, weekend and summer basis. It also lists external degree programmes, giving a description of the university which offers them as well as application details and financial-aid possibilities.

ISS Directory of International Schools (Annual)
Mea Johnston (ed.)
Available from:
International Schools Services
PO Box 5910
Princeton, New Jersey
USA 08540

This is a very comprehensive directory of all international elementary and secondary schools worldwide. Arranged according to country, it lists all international schools currently operating in that country, with details of their faculties, curriculum, fees, facilities and any special programmes that they offer. It also lists the number and nationalities of both staff and students in each school, besides indicating the ones that have boarding facilities.

D. Overseas cultural, health and low-cost travel guides

Survival Kit for Overseas Living
L. Robert Kohls
Available from:
Intercultural Press Inc
PO Box 768
Yarmouth
Maine
USA 04096

Although intended primarily for Americans, this is one of the best books on the whole process of cultural adaptation. It covers the bases of culture, the influence of values, the way stereotyping occurs, strategies for entering a country for a long-term stay, what questions to ask about a new culture, developing communication skills and managing culture shock.

The Traveller's Health Guide
Dr Anthony Turner
Available from:
Bradt Enterprises
95, Harvey Street
Cambridge
Massachussetts
USA 02140

This is an extremely informative book covering all aspects of travelling to another country and staying healthy in a new environment. It deals with all kinds of possible medical situations and gives practical advice on health care before, during and after a medical problem.

Work, Travel, Study Abroad: The Whole World Handbook
Available from:
Council on International Educational Exchange
205, East 42nd Street
New York, New York
USA 10017

Published annually, this is the best of the comprehensive guides to all the ways of finding a long-term experience overseas. Its section on study possibilities overseas covers both long and short-term opportunities and is complemented by an excellent section on the possibilities of working overseas during vacation periods.

Shoestring Guides
Tony Wheeler, et al

Available from:
Lonely Planet Publications
PO Box 2001A
Berkeley
California
USA 94702

A series of travel guides intended for the low-budget traveller, each book lists a variety of low-cost travel, accommodation and eating possibilities in each major centre, all of which have been personally vouched for by the author. It also lists the major attractions and ways in which they can visited at the lowest cost possible.

E. Useful sources of further information

1. Institute of International Education
809, United Nations Plaza
New York, NY
USA 10017

2. Association for the Advancement of International Education
Room 200, Norman Hall
College of Education
University of Florida
Gainesville
Florida
USA 32611

3. Canadian Bureau for International Education
85, Albert Street, Suite 1400
Ottawa, Ontario
Canada K1P 6A4

4. The Association of Commonwealth Universities

John Foster House
36, Gordon Square
London, WC1H 0PF
England

5. International Schools Services
PO Box 5910
Princeton, New Jersey
USA 08540

ACKNOWLEDGEMENTS

For the help I have received in writing this book, I would like to express my thanks to Bill Murtha, whose research work on the Appendix was essential, and to my son, Richard, and his girlfriend, Lauren, for their many useful suggestions on what should be included in the text. All my former students, both in Canada and overseas, also deserve a vote of thanks for the information that I have gathered over the years, as a direct result of the university and college researches we have done together.

—**Robert Barlas**

My special thanks to the many students, past and present, who have shared their experiences and insights with me on this project.

—**Guek-Cheng Pang**

ABOUT THE AUTHORS

ROBERT BARLAS

Bob (as he is usually called) was born in England and has always had wanderlust in his veins. At the age of 19, he emigrated to Canada, which has been his home—on and off—for the past 25 years.

As a teacher and guidance counsellor, Bob has worked in international education in schools all over the world—England, New Zealand, Singapore, the People's Republic of China and Sri Lanka—and has spent much of his working time there advising students who were keen to complete their education abroad. Consequently, Bob now has friends all over the world, and he loves travelling, when time permits, to visit them.

Bob is married with a son currently studying at McGill University in Montreal, Canada, and a daughter. His wife is also a teacher, specialising in remedial education. Together, the whole family has travelled to more than 60 countries—but there are still many more out there to visit!

Bob's first book for Times Editions was *Culture Shock! Sri Lanka*. He and his present co-author, Guek-Cheng Pang, have already collaborated on one other book, *Culture Shock! Canada*—and there is another in the works.

GUEK-CHENG PANG

Born in multi-racial Singapore, into a large immigrant-Chinese family that has since established its roots in the island-republic and adopted its unique culture and identity, Guek-Cheng has been an observer as well as a victim of culture shock. By training, she is a journalist and editor; by inclination, she is a student of life.

She has travelled widely and now lives in Canada with her family. Her interests include an appreciation of art, music and books, and a love of nature. When time and weather permit, she enjoys tennis, camping and skiing. Life in a new land constantly throws new challenges her way—she is always learning new living skills. She has written *Culture Shock! Canada*, a collaboration with co-author Robert Barlas, and *Cultures of the World— Canada*. When she is not writing, she works in a library, volunteers in church and is presently building her own house.

INDEX